D1276344

Starlit Paths
for Pilgrim Feet

By

Merrill F. Unger, Th.D., Ph.D., Professor at Dallas Theological Seminary, the author of "Pathway to Power," "Principles of Expository Preaching," etc.

Published by

DUNHAM PUBLISHING GOMPANY

Findlay, Ohio

Printed in U. S. A.

STARLIT PATHS FOR PILGRIM FEET

(A devotional study of the Scriptural passages which refer to the stars)

By

Merrill F. Unger

The American Revised Version used throughout.

Contents

STARLIT PATH THROUGH ETERNITY PAST

CHAPTER I   PRAISE OF THE STARS OF LIGHT 7
Divine Light and Adoring Angels 9
The Song of the Morning Stars 19

STARLIT PATH THROUGH SIN

CHAPTER II   NIGHT AND STARLIGHT 25
Darkness Invades the Light 27
Light Is Separated from Darkness 36

STARLIT PATH THROUGH TESTING

CHAPTER III   BEHOLD THE STARS! 47
The Look That Glimpses the Stars 49
Star Counting 59

STARLIT PATH THROUGH TRIAL

CHAPTER IV   STARS OF THE TWILIGHT 75
Evening Stars 77
Dusk and Darkened Stars 87

STARLIT PATH THROUGH TROUBLE

CHAPTER V   TEMPEST AND STARLESS NIGHT 101
Storms and Stars 103
Divine Judgments and Falling Stars 115

STARLIT PATH TO THE SAVIOR

CHAPTER VI   THE BRIGHT, THE MORNING STAR 131
The Star Out of Jacob 133
Dawn and the Day Star 145

STARLIT PATH TO GLORY

CHAPTER VII   THEY SHALL SHINE AS THE STARS 161
Darkness and Starlike Saints 163
When the Righteous Shine As the Stars 177

STARLIT PATH THROUGH ETERNITY PAST

Chapter One

Praise of the Stars of Light

Praise him, all his angels . . .
Praise him, all ye stars of light.
(Psa. 148:2, 3)

DIVINE LIGHT AND ADORING ANGELS

. . . God is light, and in him is no darkness at all
(1 John 1:5)
Bless Jehovah, ye his angels,
That are mighty in strength . . . (Psa. 103:20)

Night may be beautiful and romantic if illuminated by moon and stars. There is something magnificent about twilight as the glory of day fades and the splendor of dusk is revealed in the starry heavens. Poets from time immemorial have celebrated the haunting beauty of that season when nature curtains the world in shadow and rocks her creatures to sleep. In a superb ode Shelley pays tribute to Night:

> *Wrap thy form in a mantle gray,*
> *Star-inwrought!*
> *Blind with thine hair the eyes of Day;*
> *Kiss her until she be wearied out,*
> *Then wander o'er city, and, sea, and land,*
> *Touching all with thine opiate wand—*
> *Come, long-sought!*
>
> *When I arose and saw the dawn,*
> *I sighed for thee;*
> *When light rode high, and the dew was gone,*
> *And noon lay heavy on flower and tree,*
> *And weary Day turned to his rest,*
> *Lingering like an unloved guest,*
> *I sighed for thee.*

Longfellow sings superlatively in his *Hymn to the Night*:

> *I heard the trailing garments of the Night*
> *Sweep through her marble halls!*
> *I saw her sable skirts all fringed with light*
> *From the celestial walls!*
> *I felt her presence, by its spell of might,*
> *Stoop o'er me from above;*
> *The calm, majestic presence of the Night,*
> *As of the one I love . . .*

Much of the loveliness of night is due to the moon and stars—God's lustrous lamps of light hung out and placed aloft. But night, moonless and starless, wild and tempest-ridden, with its gloom unmitigated and unrelieved, is a fearful thing.

In Scripture the terms "night" and "darkness" are used figuratively to portray the woe sin has introduced into the world. Night indicates calamity and misery (Isa. 21:11; Mic. 3:6), ignorance (Job 37:19), sadness (Eccl. 5:17), wickedness (Prov. 2:13) and death (Eccl. 11:8; John 9:4). Night suggests the time for deeds of iniquity and shame (Rom. 13:12) when sinners are drunk and men are overcome by moral torpor (1 Thess. 5:7).

Whereas "night" and "darkness" are words employed figuratively in the Bible to depict the woe sin has introduced into God's universe of goodness and light, the moon and stars that illuminate the night appear as tokens of His grace and salvation operating in behalf of sinful men groping in the misery of sin and gloom.

Hence the Promised Messiah-Redeemer was foreseen as a brilliant luminary—"a star out of Jacob" (Num. 24:17). The faithful redeemed shall one day "shine as the brightness of the firmament" and as "the stars forever and ever" (Dan. 12:3). Individual believers in this age "are seen as lights (luminaries) in the world" in the midst of "a crooked and perverse generation" (Phil. 2:15). Faithful ministers of Christ are likened to brilliant "stars" securely held in the "right hand" of the Son of God (Rev. 1:16).

The Effulgent Light of God's Glory

Darkness, however, did not always exist. There was a time in eternity past when there was no night, nor need of sun, nor moon nor stars to illuminate the night, nor sin, nor misery. God alone, Who is Light (1 John 1:5), Who covers Himself "with light as with a garment" (Psa. 104:2), Who dwells "in light unapproachable" (1 Tim. 6:16), and is "the Father of lights" (James 1:17), existed in sole infinite splendor.

Before ever there were created spirits of light, before the calling into being of the serried ranks of glorious light-filled angels, before the stars and the planets were set in the vast celestial spheres, before sun and moon were hung aloft, before there was an earth with snow-capped mountains, verdant plains and sapphire seas, before there was grass, or flower, or tree, or man or beast, God *was*. "In the beginning God. . . ." (Gen. 1:1).

Before the dawn of time, inhabiting the womb of eternity, He Who is "the Alpha and the Omega . . . Who is and Who was and Who is to come, the Almighty" (Rev. 1:8), resided in the ineffably blissful solitude of His own effulgent glory. In the limitless expanse of eternity past the ever-blessed Godhead— Father, Son and Spirit—enjoyed the sublime fellowship of its own triune Being. "In the beginning was the Word, and the Word was with God, and the Word was God. The same was in the beginning with God" (John 1:1, 2).

THE DAY STAR, SON OF THE MORNING, APPEARS

How long in the endless march of a timeless eternity God dwelt alone in ineffable light in blissful communion with His own all-glorious triune Being is not known. His divine nature all the while, however, had the urge to fellowship with creatures of His hand, and His power and wisdom sought expression in bringing created beings into existence and calling worlds into space.

The first creature to emerge from the hand of the Creator was a being of dazzling light and beauty, the "day star, son of the morning" (Isa. 14:12). This radiant celestial personage, so reflected the splendor of his Maker, that even after his fall, he is still associated with the lustrous brilliance of the planet Venus, the morning star, "son of the dawn." He appears to human view as the motivating power and dynamic energy behind the splendid glory of "the king of Babylon" (Isa. 14:4-20).

This first and greatest of all God's sinless spirits of light, called by the ancients Lucifer or "Light bearer," was a reflection of the glory of his Creator. His shining upon the horizon of time was marked by the absence of shadow or any trace of darkness. He is called "the day star, son of the morning," it is true, but as yet there was no night to require stars, no gloom of sin to be dissipated into dawn. All was light, splendor and unmitigated joy, when "the day star, son of the morning," appeared in the celestial Eden.

Our hearts, although redeemed by the precious blood of Christ, yet still subject to the vexations and temptations of evil and still bound to the defilement of a sin nature and the severe limitations of a body of flesh, can scarcely imagine the glorious splendor of a sin-free universe and the high and holy converse of exalted creature with Creator. The primal communion of Creator and the first creature presents a scene of such indescribable felicity and splendid glory that it is overpowering to our sin-dimmed eyes.

We see the stars, but only through the gathering gloom. We behold the clear brilliance of Venus, the day star, but only as it is embosomed upon the sable breast of night, or momentarily, at best, as it emerges from the womb of morning.

Our blessed Lord and Savior Jesus Christ has brought us grace and foregleams of the coming glory, but meanwhile we "who have the firstfruits of the Spirit . . . groan within ourselves, waiting for our adoption, to wit, the redemption of our body" (Rom. 8:23).

Before the spectacle of the pristine splendor of a sin-free universe, fallen sin-scarred humanity finds itself far away from the light, far away from God and cynically critical and alienated, somewhat in the position of Caliban in Louis Untermeyer's famous poem, "Caliban in the Coal Mines."

> *God, we don't like to complain;*
>> *We know that the mine is no lark,*
> *But—there's the pools from the rain;*
>> *But—there's the cold and the dark.*
>
> *God, You don't know what it is—*
>> *You, in Your well-lighted sky—*
> *Watching the meteors whizz;*
>> *Warm, with a sun always by.*
>
> *God, if You had but the moon*
>> *Stuck in your cap for a lamp,*
> *Even You'd tire of it soon,*
>> *Down in the dark and the damp.*
>
> *Nothing but blackness above*
>> *And nothing that moves but the cars.*
> *God, if You wish for our love,*
>> *Fling us a handful of stars.*

But that is precisely what God has done! When there was spiritually for us "nothing but blackness above," God in Christ "flung us a handful of stars." Through the revelation of Himself and His gracious plan of salvation contained in the pages of His Holy Book, He has illuminated our darkness and won our love.

Our God has beneficently instructed us in His will and ways for our lives in the present. He has also granted us glimpses into His purposes of glory for us in the future through His prophetic Word. More than that He has permitted us to peer into His dealings with men in the flesh and to some extent, at least, has drawn aside the veil from eternity past to permit our Spirit-touched eyes to behold His own splendor and the glory of His first sinless and unfallen creatures in the angelic realms.

A CREATURE WISDOM-FILLED, PERFECT IN BEAUTY

Through the prophet Ezekiel God lifts the curtain of revelation to permit human eyes to gaze upon the uncorrupted loveliness of the Creator's first creature. Flashing before our astonished gaze is a superlative portrait of the first and mightiest of His angels, addressed under the title of the splendid ancient king of Tyre. "Thou wast in Eden, the garden of God; every precious stone was thy covering, the sardius, the topaz, the onyx, and the jasper, the sapphire, the emerald, and the carbuncle, and gold: the workmanship of thy tabrets and thy pipes was in thee; in the day that thou wast created they were prepared" (Ezek. 28:13).

Fresh from the Creator's hand and beautiful in holiness Isaiah's "day star, son of the morning" is depicted by Ezekiel darting forth iridescent rays of flashing light. He is seen shining forth now with the clear brilliance of the diamond, now with the pale green splendor of the beryl or the deeper hue of the emerald, now beaming combinations of colors of the onyx, or the lustrous blue of the sapphire, or emanating the wine or straw color or the golden yellow of the topaz, or the deep red and garnet of the carbuncle or the richness of pure gold.

God's first creature and mightiest angel was called into existence as a dazzling light-bearing being to be a diadem of praise to His Creator. "The workmanship of thy tabrets and of thy pipes was in thee; in the day that thou wast created they were prepared" (Ezek. 28:13). He had no need of an instrument of praise to laud His Creator. He himself was a coronet of praise. He was designed to advertise to all other creatures who might follow, the superbly effective power of the eternal God and His exquisite creative artistry.

THE ANGELS ARE CREATED

The appearance of the gem-studded and glorious person of Lucifer, the day star, son of the morning, in the primal Eden was the harbinger of the calling of myriads of other radiant spirits of light into being to inhabit the angelic spheres. These ethereal "spirits" of "flaming fire" (Psa. 104:4) not only reflect the power, wisdom and glory of their Creator, but ceaselessly praise Him and minister unto Him, doing "His pleasure" (Psa. 103:20, 21).

When we, the redeemed of the human race, severely limited by a physical body and subject to so much weakness, sickness and to death itself contemplate the greatness of God as manifested in the higher orders of created beings, we can only marvel at the divine condescension in stooping to rescue fallen man. When we ponder God's infinite love in giving His only begotten Son to become identified with the human race and die for sinners on a shameful cross, we can only prostrate ourselves in humble worship before our wonderful Redeemer, and say with the poet:

All hail the power of Jesus' name!
  Let angels prostrate fall;
Bring forth the royal diadem,
  And crown Him Lord of all.

Let ev'ry kindred, every tribe
  On this terrestrial ball,
To Him all majesty ascribe
  And crown Him Lord of all.

                                  Oliver Holden

Moreover, in considering angelic beings horizons must be immeasurably widened to comprehend the entire universe. No suggestion appears upon the pages of divine revelation that these incorporeal beings, unconfined by the limits of time and space and the laws that prevail in the natural sphere, are restricted to the realm of this earth, or indeed to any part of the universe. They are denizens of "the Father's house" and its "many mansions," or abodes—a beautiful figure employed by our Lord to designate nothing less than the universe with its multitudinous dwelling places (John 14:2).

Modern astronomy with its powerful telescopes has revealed the incredible vastness of the material universe and brought into the ken of men infinite worlds flung out into the unplumbed depths of the luminous heavens. In this illimitable empire of the stars, in the blaze of the light-giving bodies clustered in inconceivable profusion in the Milky Way, in the numberless celestial spheres, suns of every imaginable magnitude and of every degree of brilliance, solar systems galore, clear shining planets and satellites, which by the millions and hundreds of millions succeed each other in the shoreless starry ocean about us, our own solar system represents but a small point and our earth a tiny speck.

Are these boundless worlds about us inhabited or is our small earth alone tenanted by created beings? Men have long speculated on this age-old question. The Word of God alone speaks with authority on the subject. It discloses that angels, as an order of creatures higher than man, and not conditioned by natural laws like man, inhabit the heavenly spheres in numbers beyond human computation. These, called "the host of heaven," are composed of gradated spirits variously designated as "thrones . . . dominions . . . principalities . . . powers" (Col. 1:16), "angels and authorities" (1 Peter 3:22).

Jude asserts that angels have "their own habitation" (1:6). They are given places to dwell in as well as an "estate," or exalted holy condition to keep. This plainly indicates that angels possess abodes in the heavenlies, from which they go forth in their service for God, including ceaseless praise and adoration of their Creator, as well as ministries on behalf of the saved of the human family (Heb. 1:14).

If angelic habitation of the universe is true, this fact gives point and purpose to the vastness and splendors of the celestial spheres. These worlds of radiant light and shining beauty not only stretch limitlessly but purposefully into outer space. They constitute the "Father's house of many mansions," where our Lord is now preparing a place for His redeemed (John 14:2) and which He has furnished from the beginning of His creative activitiy as a home for the myriads of pure ethereal spirits that surround Him in adoring worship and loving service.

> *Angel voices ever singing*
> *Round the throne of light;*
> *Angel harps, forever ringing,*
> *Rest not day nor night.*
> *Thousands only live to bless Thee*
> *And confess Thee, Lord of might.*
>
> *Honor, glory, might and merit,*
> *Thine shall ever be,*
> *Father, Son, and Holy Spirit*
> *Blessed Trinity!*
> *Of the best that thou hast given*
> *Earth and heaven render Thee.*

Francis Pott

THE SONG OF THE MORNING STARS

When the morning stars sang together . . . (Job 38:7)

True song in the heart is the spontaneous outflow of fellowship with God, the Source of all joy and melody. We who have been redeemed by the blood of Christ and brought into communion with the Father know a new song, the exquisite song of redemption. How wonderful it is for us to be able to sing the praises of Him "that loveth us, and loosed us from our sins by his blood . . . and made us to be a kingdom . . . priests unto his God and Father" (Rev. 1:5, 6).

But there is an older song in the universe, the song of creation—that pure ethereal melody that has through myriads of millennia ceaselessly and spontaneously poured forth from the hearts and lips of the angelic hosts of holy creatures of God who never sinned and never knew what it is to stop praising the wisdom, majesty and power of their all-glorious Creator, who called them into joyful unbroken fellowship with Himself.

Strains of the joyful song of creation from the lips of God's unfallen creatures have floated down the corridors of time and echo in the song of the celestial living creatures in the book of the Revelation: "Holy, holy, holy, is the Lord God Almighty, who was and who is and who is to come" (Rev. 4:8).

The twenty-four elders who "give glory and honor and thanks to him that sitteth on the throne, to him that liveth forever and ever" (Rev. 4:9 also catch the exquisite melody of the song of creation as they "fall down before him that sitteth on the throne . . . and worship him that liveth forever," as they sing: "Worthy art thou, our Lord and our God, to receive the glory and the honor and the power; for thou didst create all things, and because of thy will they were, and were created" (Rev. 4:10, 11).

THE SONG IS BORN

But the song was born ages before in the hearts of the holy angels. It sprang spontaneously from contact and communion of the first creatures with their Creator. It flowed forth in immeasurable fulness, pure and unsullied, when the world was young. Its golden melody resounded through space when the foundation of the earth was set, when its expanse was stretched out, when it was hung upon nothing and its cornerstone was laid (Job 38:1-6). It was in celebration of this grand event "the morning stars sang together and all the sons of God shouted for joy" (Job 38:7).

The morning stars sang together! All "the sons of God" shouted for joy to herald earth's creation morn! "The morning stars" represent Lucifer, "the day star, son of the morning" (Isa. 14:12) and other bright stars, his peers. Joining the choir of these angels of higher rank and more radiant glory were "the sons of God" or angels of lesser rank and lustre.

As the heavens are dotted with multitudinous stars in the night, which gradually fade out of sight till only the brightest remain when dawn begins to suffuse the sky with light, and these so-called "morning stars" in turn vanish as the sun rises, so God's heavenly host is gradated in ranks of glory. But the vast symphony that welcomed a new orb hung in space was composed of a full choir. Not merely "the morning stars" but the lesser stars—the vast myriads of angels.

As each tiny orb of light in the clear nocturnal heavens adds its bit of lustre, which together with the superb radiance of a Venus, a Canopus or an Orion make up the magnificence of the night skies, so all the sons of God added their harmonies to the song of the resplendent "morning stars" to celebrate earth's glorious birthday morn.

A Golden Orb Is Hung in Space

What a morn it was when God fashioned the earth! It was a small sphere in comparison with some of the other planets and stars set out in the celestial expanse, but it was made exquisite in beauty to be Lucifer's abode and the home of other bright spirits of light. Upon it the Creator lavished His wisdom and skill.

Fresh from the Creator's hand, the new world,

floating in the light and glory of its Maker, must have been a vast Edenic garden with sprawling plains, verdant hills, fruitful valleys and majestic mountains mirrored in sapphire seas. The sight of the new sphere radiating God's glory signalled the adoring song of all created beings. The laying of its foundation marked a vast celestial celebration. The setting of its cornerstone called forth the golden harmonies of vast angelic choirs.

What a scene of indescribable grandeur! What an occasion of transcendent joy! Jubilating hosts of ethereal spirits of light! Singing morning stars! Shouting sons of God! A new world born! A resplendent manifestation of divine power! An exquisite exhibition of worship and radiant holiness of the creature without a trace of sin! A blissful event of unmitigated joy unspoiled by a single tear! An interstellar symphony without a minor note!

> *Embosomed in celestial light,*
>   *Fashioned with supernal grace,*
> *Created by God's matchless might,*
>   *A golden orb is hung in space.*
>
> *Suspended in an ocean blue,*
>   *Floating in a starry sea,*
> *Festooned with the rainbow's hue—*
>   *A product of God's artistry.*
>
> *Enveloped in seraphic song*
>   *Enwombed for illustrious birth,*
> *Encircled by angelic throng,*
>   *God laid the cornerstone of earth.*

Enraptured hosts with jubilant praise
Attend the grand nativity
Serried heavenly spirits raise
An interstellar symphony.

Merrill F. Unger

But the new planet was not only made exquisite in beauty to be Lucifer's abode. In the divine counsels it was also constituted dear to the heart of the Creator as man's future home and the place where the Son of God was to become incarnate and die on a cross for the sin of a ruined race.

To us who have been redeemed by the blood of Christ and who look back at creation's morn through Gethsemane's dark night and Calvary's shadows, the greatest marvel of all is not the calling into being of a new sphere with accompaniment of seraphic song, but that He Who made that world and all the worlds in the universe, the mighty Christ of God, was He Who was cradled on a virgin's heart and died for sinners on a cursed tree.

The Maker of the Universe
As man for man was made a curse;
The claims of laws which He had made
Unto the uttermost He paid.
His holy fingers made the bough
Where grew the thorns that crowned His brow;
The nails that pierced His hands were mined
In secret places He designed.

He made the forests whence there sprung
The tree on which His body hung;
He died upon a cross of wood
Yet made the hill on which it stood!
The sky which darkened o'er His head
By Him above the earth was spread;
The sun which hid from Him its face
By His decree was poised in space!

The spear which spilt His precious blood
Was tempered in the fires of God;
The grave in which His form was laid
Was hewed in rocks His hands had made!
The throne on which He now appears
Was His from everlasting years!
But a new glory crowns His brow
And every knee to Him shall bow!

STARLIT PATH THROUGH SIN

Chapter Two

Night and Starlight

Who giveth . . . the stars for a light by night (Jer. 31:35).

DARKNESS INVADES THE LIGHT

When I made . . . thick darkness a swaddling band . . .
(Job 38:9)
. . . And darkness was upon the face of the deep . . .
(Gen. 1:2).

The joyous light that filled the pristine sinless universe and radiated from angels and morning stars and merged into mighty symphony of song at the laying of earth's cornerstone was not destined to continue undisturbed. The infinitely wise Creator, in endowing his creatures with freedom of will and the prerogative of self-determining choice, allowed the possibility at least that some might choose the wrong way and thereby introduce sin, darkness and misery into His perfect and sinless creation.

Divine wisdom, however, knew that the joy of fellowship with the Creator maintained against solicitation to apostasy and disloyalty would be a deeper and more enlightened emotion. Light appearing against the background of darkness would be more resplendent. Holiness shining out against the sombreness of sin would be more attractive. The majesty of the major key would be more pronounced by contrast with the minor note. A smile would radiate all the more beautifully through tears. The steel girder supporting the towering skyscraper would be made strong for its task by fierce tempering heat.

The all-wise Creator knew that the sorrow and
pain caused by sin would elicit divine compassion and
that there would be men, redeemed by Christ, who in
the fierce battle against evil would be constrained to
direct noble petitions to the throne of grace—requests
like those Carl Sandberg calls "Prayers of Steel:"

> *Lay me on an anvil, O God.*
> *Beat me and hammer me into a steel spike.*
> *Drive me into the girders that hold a skyscraper together.*
> *Take red-hot rivets and fasten me into the central girders.*
> *Let me be the great nail holding a skycraper*
>   *through the blue nights into white stars.*

In the divine economy, by permitting the introduction of sin into His creation, God not only provided opportunity for men to pray such noble prayers
but made full provision for their answer.

How long, however, the unsullied light of a sinless universe and the unbroken joy of myriads of unfallen ethereal spirits continued is unrevealed in Holy
Scripture. It may have been an indefinitely extended
period. Ages upon ages of blissful harmony may have
been enjoyed by the Creator and the sin-free creature
before the dawn of time, when in eternity past "a
thousand years" were "but as yesterday when it is past,
and as a watch in the night" (Psa. 90:4).

Sin Is Born in a Sinless Universe

The prophet Isaiah under inspiration records the
tremendous scene when sin made its dismal entrance
into a sin-free universe and began its tragic career.
The ancient seer recounts how evil came into being
in an act of deliberate, wilful and intelligent trans-

gression on the part of Lucifer in the face of the full glow of light and the unobscured recognition of the divine goodness and perfection: "How art thou fallen from heaven, *O day-star, son of the morning!* how art thou cut down to the ground, that didst lay low the nations! And thou saidst in thy heart, I will ascend into heaven, I will exalt my throne above the stars of God; and I will sit upon the mount of congregation, in the uttermost parts of the north; I will ascend above the heights of the clouds; I will make myself like the Most High" (Isa. 14:12-14).

Concisely the crime of Satan is stated to be to make himself "like the Most High." This sinister determination involved in its ultimate outworking nothing less than an attempt to dethrone the Almighty Himself. Lifted up because of his beauty, carried away with the high privilege of guarding the divine throne, the "Covering Cherub" was driven by sin to strike at the very throne he was set to protect.

Engendered in the heart of the creature, sin immediately began to manifest its malignity, its remorseless cruelty and the terrible fate toward which it drives all those who are caught in its clutches. The history of iniquity whether in its tragic outworking among the angelic hosts or in its terrible ravages in the human race, is the same. It snares its victim and then mercilessly destroys him.

One of the most famous pieces of sculpture from antiquity, "The Lacoön," discovered in 1506 and now among the art treasures of the Vatican, furnishes a powerful illustration of the ensnaring and ruinous power of sin. With almost agonizing naturalness this magnificent object of art represents the famous incident immortalized by Virgil, of a son of Priam, who, seeing his two sons caught by a serpent, rushes to their aid, but is himself caught in its toils, and with them is slowly crushed to death.

What a stupendous event it was when the first creature was caught in the toils of evil and "the mystery of iniquity" (2 Thess. 2:7) began its relentless inworking, exerting its baneful pressure upon the holy unfallen creatures in God's universe. Satan's sin is set forth as consisting of five rebellious *I wills* uttered against the divine will, each more wicked than the other. Tremendous was the crisis in the universe when the first repudiation of God took place. Awful is the fact that the defection occurred in the heart of the highest and brightest of the angelic beings. Sobering it is to discover the quintessence of that sin was pride (1 Tim. 3:6), the insatiable desire to rise above the sphere in which the creature was created and above the purpose and service assigned to him.

This aspect of Satan's defection appears in the first of the five unholy declarations that express the full sweep of his wicked ambition: *"I will ascend into heaven."* In his use of the term "heaven" Satan evidently means the third or highest heaven, where God Himself and the redeemed have their abode (2 Cor. 12:1-4). Lucifer, like other angels, has his domicile in the second heaven, comprising the unfathomable realms of the starry spheres. Although his exalted activities give him access to both the earth and the higher planes (Job. 1:6; Ezek. 28:14), yet his overweening spirit of self-promotion determined that his abode should be more exalted than that sphere appointed him by his Creator.

"I will exalt my throne above the stars of God." Although appointed to guard the Creator's throne, Satan coveted a throne of his own, from which to rule "the stars of God." He desired dominion more especially over the angelic hosts (Rev. 12:3, 4), but his inordinate ambition most certainly extended to their abode in the vast starry worlds as well.

"I will sit upon the mount of congregation, in the uttermost parts of the north." This arrogant pretension evidently expresses determination to receive Messianic recognition. The term "mount" is frequently used of the seat of divine government in the millennial earth (Isa. 2:1-4). "The mount of congregation" connects the governmental administration with Israel, whose meeting place with God in the wilderness is many times called "the tabernacle of the congregation (Exod. 27:21). Against Satanic opposition to God's program for Christ's earth-rule over Israel and the nations, the divine word is:

> *Yet have I set my king*
> *Upon my holy hill of Zion* (Psa. 2:6).

This "holy hill of Zion" in Psalm 48 is characterized as "the city of our God, in his holy mountain." It is thus described with particular reference to its millennial character when it will be the world's capital and the center of the divine government:

> *Beautiful in elevation, the joy of the whole earth*
> *Is mount Zion, on the sides of the north,*
> *The city of the great King* (Psa. 48:2).

Satan's evil plan is thus to oppose "the great King"
and himself arrogate his regal honors.

"I will ascend above the heights of the clouds."
The meaning of Satan's assumption in this declaration is evidently his determination to take to himself
glory which belongs to God alone.   Many times in
Scripture, clouds are associated with the revelation of
the divine glorious Presence.   When Aaron spoke to
the Israelites "they looked toward the wilderness, and,
behold, the glory of Jehovah appeared in the cloud"
(Exod. 16:10).   It was "in the cloud" that God appeared upon the mercy seat (Lev. 16:2).   "Clouds and
darkness" are said to be round about the divine Presence (Psa. 97:2).   Christ will come at His second advent "on the clouds of heaven with power and great
glory" (Matt. 24:30).   Satan's "man of sin" will oppose
and exalt himself "against all that is called God or that
is worshipped" (2 Thess. 2:4), as Satan himself has
purposed to do.

"I will make myself like the Most High."   This
is Satan's supreme ambition—by his own pride and
rebellion to make himself what his Creator never intended any creature to be—"like the Most High."
This exalted personage did not mean he was determined to make himself "like Jehovah," the ineffable
self-existent One.   For the creature to attempt   such
an impossibility would be pointless.   What Satan did
determine was to usurp authority in heaven and upon
earth which only rightly belongs to "the Most High."

This glorious title designates God as "possessor of heaven and earth" (Gen. 14:19, 22), not only by virtue of creation, but now, in the case of the earth, by virtue of redemption as well.

In seeking relentlessly to gain authority over heaven and earth, the terrible evil of Satan's sin is advertised as an inveterate unwillingness on the part of the creature to remain in the position in which he was placed by the Creator. To be "like the Most High" Satan undertook the permanent role of imitator of God and counterfeiter of the divine plans and purposes.

> *Lord of all being, enthroned afar,*
> *Thy splendor shown in the Day Star;*
> *Angel of beauty, endued with light*
> *Created by Thy glorious might.*
>
> *Creature gem-studded, dazzling to see,*
> *Worshipping, serving, loving but Thee,*
> *Leaving his High and holy estate,*
> *Introduced sin and terrible hate.*
>
> *Lord of all being, Ancient of Days,*
> *Girded with splendor, panoplied with praise,*
> *Teach us the bliss in Thee only found,*
> *Thy glories may we ever resound.*
>
> Merrill F. Unger

DARKNESS COVERS THE DEEP

Satan's apostasy introduced night into God's moral universe. Previous to the fall of the "day star, son of the dawn" and his angelic hosts, dazzling light unobscured by even a trace of shadow, flooded the universe and clothed all God's holy and radiant creatures.

But when unrighteousness was found in the first creature who had been perfect from the day he was created, he was "cast as profane out of the mountain of God" and destroyed "from the midst of the stones of fire" (Ezek. 28:15-17).

Satan's beauty was corrupted. His glory was tarnished. His wisdom was defiled. The earth over which he and his angelic satellites were placed and in connection with which he rebelled, was visited with divine judgment and reduced from a paradise of Edenic splendor to a state of indescribable confusion.

To advertise to the universe the heinousness of sin, the globe was contorted and twisted into an uninhabitable chaotic mass. The terse and terrible story is told in the opening chapter of divine revelation. "And the earth was waste and void; and *darkness was upon the face of the deep . . .*" (Gen. 1:2).

Darkness upon the face of the deep! Chaos invading God's perfect order! These are the scars of Satan's sin left in the material world. The earth, which was directly concerned with the beginning of evil and which was apparently the place where it was actually born in the heart of Lucifer, was in consequence, to display the results of it in being convulsed, broken up and curtained in inpenetrable gloom and confusion.

Sin has never produced any other result. Wherever it is practiced it eventuates in anarchy and darkness. It engenders confusion and misery. It gives birth to pain, sorrow and every conceivable woe.

Sin has never made one heart tender, never shed

one tear of pity or compassion, never lifted one fallen soul, never helped the needy or set one erring foot in the way of righteousness, never shown one person the path of peace or kindled one spark of love.

Sin has broken hearts, wrecked homes, orphaned children, oppressed the weak, destroyed empires and brought down mighty men to the dust. Sin has filled people with selfishness, ignorance and darkness and drowned them in destruction and perdition. It has corrupted angels and ruined men. It changed an archangel into an arch devil. It transformed multitudes of pure ethereal spirits of light into unclean, pernicious demons of darkness. It reduced an originally Edenic earth to indescribable disorder and mantled it in dark shadows and filled it with fearful waste.

This globe still bears evidences of divine judgment against the first rebellion embedded deep in its crust. Jagged boulders, displaced, bizarrely tilted rock strata and strange geological formations attest a very ancient gigantic physical upheaval. Even though the Creator in His recreative work upon the earth preparatory to its habitation by man, brought order out of the confusion, He has nevertheless permitted traces of the disorder caused by the original sin to remain, not only by overruling evil to give the earth a wilder, more fantastic beauty, but also by these mute mementoes written in rocky gorge and yawning chasm, to remind men of the awfulness of revolt against God.

And men need to be constantly reminded of the fearfulness of sin and the terrible ruin it brings upon the creature. They need perpetually to realize that sin is no respecter of persons. It destroys the wise and wealthy as well as the ignorant and the poor. It lays low the mighty hero as well as the craven coward. Alexander the Great could conquer the world of his day. However, the great warrior was no match for sin when he yielded to its enticements, but prematurely ended his days at the peak of his career, in a drunken carousel in Babylon.

As sin among the angelic hosts gave birth to chaos and darkness, so men are blinded by iniquity and stumble on in spiritual gloom and do not come into the light until they embrace Christ, "the light of the world" (John 8:12).

> *Ye dwellers of darkness with sin-blinded eyes,*
> *The Light of the world is Jesus;*
> *Go, wash at His bidding, and light will arise,*
> *The Light of the world is Jesus.*
>
> *Come to the Light, tis shining for thee;*
> *Sweetly the Light has dawned upon me.*
> *Once I was blind, but now I can see;*
> *The Light of the world is Jesus.*
>
> **P. P. Bliss**

LIGHT IS SEPARATED FROM DARKNESS

. . . And God divided the light from the darkness
(Gen. 1:3)
What communion hath light with darkness?
(2 Cor. 6:14).

The chief manifestation of the disorder sin introduced in the material universe was not only that darkness came into existence, but also that it invaded and contaminated the light. The result was chaos and confusion. The grand signal that the all-wise Creator, the "Father of lights," with whom there "can be no variation, neither shadow that is cast by turning" (James 1:17), was moving in grace to undo the disorder of sin and to repair the damage it had wrought in the material universe, was His sublime declaration on the first of the seven days of recreation, "Let there be light" (Gen. 1:3).

It is not declared that God created light. He merely said, "Let there be light" (Gen. 1:3). By His omnipotent Word, light with which He had always clothed Himself, and with which He had resplendently adorned Lucifer and all the "angels of light," and which illuminated the jubilant scene when the morning stars and all the sons of God celebrated the primeval creation of the earth, was rendered visible, insofar as the judgment-ridden gloom-enshrouded earth was concerned. The dense accumulations of fogs and impenetrable mists that had blanketed the chaos with deep shadows were broken up, permitting light to shine through.

THE LIGHT IS GOOD

"And God saw the light, *that it was good . . .*" (Gen. 1:4). He who is perfect in symmetry and infinite in beauty and who is "not the author of confusion" (I Cor. 14:33), must begin any creative or recreative work by banishing chaos. He Who Himself "is light" and in Whom "is no darkness at all" (1 John 1:5), in accordance with His own all-glorious nature must pronounce the light good. He must deal with darkness, rigidly confining it, and taking steps to banish it eventually.

In calling forth light, it is important to note that God did not annihilate the darkness that enshrouded the chaotic earth. He did not banish it, because in His all-wise purpose neither sin nor sinners were to be annihilated. Darkness was to remain as a reminder of sin and the presence of rebellion in the moral universe. But there was a higher purpose. In God's plan to permit sin and sinners to enter His originally sinless universe the divine wisdom and goodness would overrule the evil for good.

The presence of sin in the world would be used to call forth the marvels of God's redemptive grace toward men. In the case of the redeemed the finest and strongest character would be developed by struggle against the pressures and temptations of evil. God's children would be made to discover that the grandest disclosures of God's mercy and the greatest appreciation of God's love and power would result in the struggle against pain, sorrow, sin and death.

God knew that the testimony of His redeemed children would be that the most precious lessons of life would be learned in the school of tears and trials in a world of sin and woe.

> *I learn, as the years roll onward*
> *And I leave the past behind,*
> *That much I had counted sorrow*
> *But proves that God is kind;*
> *That many a flower I had longed for*
> *Had hidden a thorn of pain,*
> *And many a rugged by-path*
> *Led to fields of ripened grain.*

The clouds that cover the sunshine
    They cannot banish the sun;
And the earth shines out the brighter
    When the weary rain is done.
We must stand in the deepest shadow
    To see the clearest light;
And often through wrong's own darkness
    Comes the weary strength of right.

The sweetest rest is at even,
    After a wearisome day,
When the heavy burden of labor
    Has taken our strength away;
And those who have never known sorrow
    Can not know the infinite peace
That falls on the troubled spirit
    When it sees at last release.

We must live through the dreary winter
    If we would value the spring;
And the woods must be cold and silent
    Before the robins sing.
The flowers must be buried in darkness
    Before they can bud and bloom,
And the sweetest, warmest sunshine
    Comes after the storm and gloom.

Anonymous

Although God did not annihilate darkness and sin, He did what His infinitely holy being demanded. He "divided the light from the darkness." At the very commencement of His recreative work He demonstrated that only as righteousness is rigidly differentiated from unrighteousness and obedience to the divine will from disobedience can cosmos be brought out of chaos.

The essential moral distinction involved in the

divine separation of the light from darkness constitutes the basis not only of God's character, but under-
lies the beginning of His recreative work in the earth
and His regenerative work in man as well. It is the
foundation of all right conduct in the world and
originates in the Creator of the universe. "Howbeit,
the firm foundation of God standeth, having this seal,
The Lord knoweth them that are his: and, Let every
one that nameth the name of the Lord depart from
unrighteousness" (2 Tim. 2:19).

Biologists describe an insect which, though im-
mersed in water, yet never touches the water. Sur-
rounded by the element, yet the element never pene-
trates to the insect itself. The reason for this wonder
in nature is that the little creature carries its own atmosphere with it. Enveloped first in this atmosphere, it can bid the other element defiance and,
though submerged in it, is untouched by it.

God expects us to be so in contact with Him that
we shall carry about with us the secret atmosphere of
communion, and then, though in the midst of darkness and sin, we shall live in the light and remain
without blemish, unspotted by the world. Only in
this way can we enjoy fellowship with a holy God.

"And God called the light Day, and the darkness
he called Night" (Gen. 1:5). The Creator would
very clearly have the difference between light and
darkness perpetuated by the distinctive names he as-
signs to each. To ignore such distinctions or to break
them down is to court anarchy and reduce the beauty
of holiness to the chaos of sin.

Since God first called forth light to shine upon earth's confused gloom, and separated that light from darkness, the divine pronouncement has always been: "Woe to them that call evil good, and good evil; that put darkness for light, and light for darkness; that put bitter for sweet, and sweet for bitter!" (Isa. 5:20).

The sphere and the time of the appearance of light as a manifestation of God Himself (evidently not the light of the sun, which had not yet appeared as an earth luminary) was called Day. The realm and the period of darkness as a withdrawing of God's manifested presence and a figure of the evil of sin, were called night.

NIGHT IS ILLUMINATED BY LIGHT

God permitted the darkness, but separated it from the light. But the all-wise gracious Creator did more than this! He illuminated the darkness with light. "And God said, Let there be lights in the firmament of heaven to divide the day from the night; and let them be for signs, and for seasons, and for days and years: and let them be for lights in the firmament of heaven to give light upon the earth; and it was so" (Gen. 1:14, 15).

The darkness which sin brought into the universe was not to be unmitigated. In the renewed heavens and earth, luminaries were to beautify, adorn and illuminate the firmament, and mark the unending succession of days, months and years with their ever-changing seasons. First and foremost, however, they were to be for "signs," that is, celestial monuments or symbols memorializing the divine grace and goodness and reminding man that, even before the creation and fall of the human race, God had moved to alleviate darkness and provide the light of his grace to illuminate the night sin had introduced.

"And God made the two great lights; the greater light to rule the day, and the lesser light to rule the night: *he made the stars also.* And God set them in the firmament of heaven to give light upon the earth, and to rule over the day and over the night, and to divide the light from the darkness . . . " (Gen. 1:16-18).

The greatest luminary of the earth, the sun, which in the strength of its brilliance is able completely to dispel the darkness, signifies Him Who is called "The sun of righteousness" (Mal. 4:2), and who, as the supreme manifestation of God's redeeming love, is "the light of the world" (John 8:12). When Christ shines into our hearts, He gives "the light of the knowledge of the glory of God" (2 Cor. 4:6), and we who were "once darkness" became "light in the Lord" Eph. 5:8). As the sun arising in flaming splendor upon the eastern horizon banishes the deep gloom of night and ushers in the glory of a new day, so Christ Jesus arising "with healing in His beams" in the believer's heart, heralds the dawning of God's salvation from sin, and the beginning of a new life and hope in the human soul.

The lesser luminary of the earth which derives its light by reflection from the sun, the moon, symbolizes the church as it radiates a glory wholly derived from Christ. The church, moreover, belongs in a moral and dispensational sense to the night or period prior to the second advent when Christ will appear in the distinctive character as "the sun of righteousness" to dispell the darkness and bring in the resplendent millennial day. Now Christ shines, but "in the darkness," and He is comprehended only by faith (John 1:4, 5).

"He made the stars also"—millions upon millions of these bright lamps to illumine the darkness when no other light relieves the blackness of night. Belonging in a special sense to the night and shining with clear sparkling lustre in the nocturnal skies, the stars represent individual believers, who "are seen as lights (luminaries) in the world, holding forth the word of life" (Phil. 2:15, 16). Clothed in the splendor of Christ's holiness, and radiant in "the beauty of the Lord" (Psa. 90:17), true believers rise star-like on the night of surrounding sin. Under this figure they are trophies of God's grace in the darkness of this present age, as the stars were manifestations of the Creator's goodness in the day they were made to shed forth their twinkling light to lessen the darkness of the primeval night.

RADIANT STARS OF HOPE

The refashioning of the chaotic earth into a sphere of Edenic paradise for man's abode was followed by the fall of the primeval pair and the entrance of woe into the human family. The night of sin settled down upon unfallen man's brief day. With sin came shame, sorrow, pain and death. The long history of human heartbreak and tragedy began.

The ground is cursed with thorns and thistles.

Man is afflicted with labor as he wrestles with a hostile earth, till he returns in death to the dust from which he was taken. Anger, lust, murder and sin's whole foul brood break out in man's heart and manifest themselves in his deeds. The first child of the human race becomes the brutal murderer of his own brother. The descendants of this first killer became notorious for crime and violence alongside their advance in the arts and crafts of civilization (Gen. 4:16-24).

By the time of the flood the wickedness of man was so great "that every imagination of the thoughts of his heart was only evil continually" (Gen. 5:6), and God had to destroy the earth and man upon it with a flood, preserving only a small righteous remnant from the universal violence and corruption that prevailed.

But this dark night was not unrelieved by starlight. God had His messengers of light shining in the darkest gloom. In the moment of supreme tragedy when man disobeyed and ate of the forbidden tree, a glistening star of hope shone out resplendently against the sombre background of man's sin, giving promise of the Coming Redeemer, "the daystar" (1 Peter 1:19) "the bright and morning star" (Rev. 22:16). The divine word to the serpent-tempter proclaimed the ultimate victory of God's grace over man's sin, and projected its reassuring radiance over the intervening centuries of human misery and woe: "I will put enmity between thee and the woman, and between thy seed and her seed: he shall bruise thy head, and thou shalt bruise his heel" (Gen. 3:15).

From that fateful moment marking man's fall and the manifestation of God's promised grace, the one star of hope has become a whole sky full of stars in the Messianic promises recorded in revealed truth, and each succeeding one has become brighter and clearer than its predecessor. The Messianic promises vouchsafed to Abraham (Gen. 12:1-3) are more specific than those given to Noah (Gen. 9:26, 27). Likewise those given to David (Psa. 22;110) and Isaiah (9:6; 53:1-12) are more far-reaching than those given to Moses. Micah even names Messiah's birthplace (Mic. 5:2) and Malachi hails Him and the Bringer-in of the glad millennial day (Mal. 4:2).

A whole cluster of redemptive promises found fulfilment at the birth, death, resurrection and ascension of our blessed Lord at this first advent. Other great galaxies of promises still await their consummation at the second advent of our Lord as "the bright and morning star," the harbinger of the dawn, in connection with His coming for His own, and as the "sun of righteousness" in relation to the establishment of the future millennial kingdom over Israel.

Meanwhile, however dark the shadow of affliction or sorrow may be for the child of God, *night is always coupled with starlight,* and the eye of faith is not to *look at* the night but *for* the stars! No matter how black and tempestuous the night, the stars are always there! They are there as bright and gleaming as ever, though for the moment obscured by tempest and trial. Above the storm's fury they shine just as radiantly and twinkle just as peacefully as on the stillest, clearest night.

The Stars are there!
  Above the shroud
  Of stormy cloud,
  And tempest loud,
  Above the din
  Of human sin,
Shining with a radiance rare.

The Stars are there!
  Faith's eye can sight
  God's lamps of light,
  In darkest night
  Hung out in space
  Betokening grace,
Pointing to the city fair.

The Stars are there!
  God's words sublime
  From Book divine,
  As lights that shine;
  To show the way
  To endless day,
Freeing men from sin's despair.

      Merrill F. Unger

STARLIT PATH THROUGH TESTING

Chapter Three

Behold the Stars!

. . . Behold the . . . stars, how high they are. (Job 22:12)

THE LOOK THAT GLIMPSES THE STARS

Look now toward heaven and number the stars . . .
(Gen. 15:5)

Since moral and spiritual night settled over the race as a result of the fall and the entrance of sin into the human heart, God's pilgrim people of all ages have had to face periods of protracted darkness. During such nightime experiences of trial and temptation, the only way of deliverance has been the upward look. So dark and tempestuous has been the night, so cloud-obscured and starless the heavens, so apparently hopeless the situation, that only the skyward gaze to God alone could bring assurance of help and the confidence that the starry lamps of God's promises were still shining aloft, behind and above the stormy blast.

THE EXPERIENCE OF THE STARLESS NIGHT

The ancient bard of Israel had a similar experience of starless night. At such a time he could look to God alone in his trouble and know that He Who was the omnipotent Creator of all things was able to meet his need, when all other helpers failed:

I will lift up mine eyes unto the mountains:
From whence shall my help come?
My help cometh from Jehovah,
Who made heaven and earth.

> *He will not suffer thy foot to be moved:*
> *He that keepeth thee will not slumber.*
> *Behold, he that keepeth Israel*
> *Will neither slumber nor sleep.*
> *Jehovah is thy keeper:*
> *Jehovah is thy shade upon thy right hand.*
> *The sun shall not smite thee by day,*
> *Nor the moon by night.*
> *Jehovah will keep thee from all evil;*
> *He will keep thy soul.*
> *Jehovah will keep thy going out and thy coming in*
> *From this time forth and forevermore* (Psa. 121:1-8).

The Lord's singer in Psalm 46 evidently lifted up his "song in the night" in the midst of a particularly dark situation. But he saw the stars!

> *God is our refuge and strength,*
> *A very present help in trouble.*
> *Therefore will we not fear, though the earth do change*
> *And though the mountains be shaken into the heart of the seas.*
> *Though the waters thereof roar and be troubled,*
> *Though the mountains tremble with the swelling thereof.*
> 　*Selah.*
>
> *There is a river, the streams whereof make glad the city of*
> 　*God*
> *The holy place of the tabernacles of the Most High.*
> *God is in the midst of her; she shall not be moved:*
> *God will keep her, and that right early.*
> *The nations raged, the kingdoms were moved:*
> *He uttered His voice, the earth melted.*
> *Jehovah of hosts is with us;*
> *The God of Jacob is our refuge* (Psa. 46:1-7).

Abraham as "the friend of God" (James 2:23), the father of all who believe, "who in hope believed against hope" (Rom. 4:18), often found himself tried and tested in a night-time experience. The darkness appeared impenetrable. The hand of God, graciously revealed for his encouragement and help, and illuminating his darkened sky with the lamp of light and promise, was the only hope of God's ancient servant.

The matter of Sarah's childlessness in particular was a severe trial to Abraham. The fact that he had no son of his own, and hence no real heir, was a deep anxiety to the patriarch, as it is universally among peoples of Eastern lands. "O Lord Jehovah, what wilt thou give me, seeing I go childless, and he that shall be possessor of my house is Eliezer of Damascus?" (Gen. 15:3).

LIGHT FOR THE STARLESS NIGHT

As Abraham faces the sombre fact that his servant is his heir since God had given him no progeny, the divine light begins to break upon the scene. The Lord appears to his servant in a vision with words of great encouragement: "Fear not, Abram, I am thy shield and thy exceeding great reward" (Gen. 15:1). It was a grand intimation of that superlatively multiplied recompense of Abraham's faith centering not so much in the possession of the Promised Land, but focussing its emphasis in the glorious far-reaching salvation to come through the Promised Seed.

"This man shall not be thine heir, but he that shall come forth out of thine own bowels shall be thine heir" (Gen. 15:3). These words are staggering in their scope, and flashed upon the patriarch's eyes, accustomed to the night of his experience, are dazzling. Like one suddenly emerging from the shadows of a dark room is blinded by the noonday sun, Abraham is dazed.

With infinite graciousness his divine Friend adapts the promise to the focus of Abraham's eye of faith and to the night of his experience. "And he brought him forth abroad, and said, Look now toward heaven, and number the stars, if thou be able to number them; and he said unto him, So shall thy seed be" (Gen. 15:5).

The glory of the promise, like the blazing sun of day, is accommodated to the night and the softer lustre of the stars. *"Look now toward heaven!"* That is the only direction to look—upward to God—if one is to see the stars of His promises and the light He gives in the darkest night. One may look around or down provided only the light He gives is reflected in people or circumstances around us, as a clear mountain lake may mirror the infinite meadows of heaven and their starry train, as we look down upon it or around upon it on a clear moonless night.

When we lift our eyes upward and Godward, we find the lamps of God's love begin shining forth like the stars of the twilight as night falls.

> *Silently one by one*
> *In the infinite meadows of heaven*
> *Blossomed the lovely stars,*
> *The forget-me-nots of the angels.*

Abraham looked heavenward toward God and glimpsed the multitudinous stars of God in the Palestinian heavens. "And he believed in Jehovah; and he reckoned it to him for righteousness" (Gen. 15:6). The upward look is not only a star-envisioning experience,

but a faith-producing exercise as well. It inspired justi-
fying faith in God's ancient servant, as it does in every
servant of God.

The upward look of the patriarch in this night-
time experience with the starlight flooding his heart,
brings with it the reminder of another such event involving God's gracious light-imparting intervention in
a time of darkness and testing. And the Lord said
unto him, "I am Jehovah that brought thee out of Ur
of the Chaldees, to give thee this land to inherit it"
(Gen. 15:7).

The call to leave his ancestral home in the wealthy
and famous Southern Babylonian city of Ur for an
unknown and uncertain destination in Palestine appeared like a leap in the dark. It involved going out
"not knowing whither he went" (Heb. 11:8). But
God's saint was vouchsafed light in the darkness.
"The God of glory appeared unto our father Abraham, when he was in Mesopotamia, before he dwelt
in Haran" (Acts 7:2). Moreover, it was the voice
of "the God of glory" that gave the command, "Get
thee out of thy land and from thy kindred, and come
into the land which I shall show thee" (Acts 7:3).

PUTTING ONE'S HAND IN THE HAND OF GOD

In obeying the divine voice, Abraham became like
the man who put his hand in the hand of God in
Minnie Louise Haskins poem, *God Knows*: "And I
said to the man who stood at the gate of the year:
'Give me a light that I may tread safely into the unknown.' And he replied, 'Go out into the darkness
and put your hand into the hand of God. That shall

be to you better than the light and safer than a known way.' So I went forth, and finding the hand of God, trod gladly into the night. And he led me toward the hills and the breaking of the day in the lone East."

No wonder the darkness disappeared and unbelief vanished as the patriarch left Ur. No wonder the night became lustrous with the light of God's love and presence as he put his hand in the hand of God. No wonder the long trek to Canaan became a path as luminous and glorious as the Milky Way instead of a trackless and fearful desert wandering, eventuating in disappointment and death.

But the night is deceptive, and even in the case of God's pilgrims who have seen it made splendid by the revelation of God's light and love, darkness has a tendency to settle down upon them, blotting out the lamps of God and enshrouding them in gloom and discouragement. This was Abraham's temptation *in* the land. His faith had been magnificent to leave Ur of the Chaldeans *for* the land. But once in the land the darkness begins to settle upon his vision and his anxious question becomes "O Lord Jehovah, whereby shall I know that I shall inherit it?" (Gen. 15:8).

"Whereby shall I know that I shall inherit it?" *Because God said so!* "And he said unto him, I am Jehovah that brought thee out of Ur of the Chaldees, *to give thee this land to inherit it*" (v. 7). But when the darkness falls, it threatens to blot out the promises of God's Word from our vision. We then need a visible demonstration of the power and efficacy of that Word to give us added light in the night to strengthen our faith and an unusually bright star to penetrate the deep gloom.

An Extraordinary Exhibition of God's Presence

God gave such a special light to Abraham to prepare him for a dismally dark experience, directing him to offer a sacrifice of five different animals. All of these animals—the heifer, the goat, the ram, the turtle dove and the pigeon—are mentioned later in the Levitical law as sacrifices typical of Christ. Abraham divided the heifer, goat and ram "in the midst and laid each half over against the other: but the birds," as in Leviticus 1:17, "divided he not" (Gen. 15:10).

This ancient method of making a covenant, in this instance, speaks of God's agreement with the patriarch, executed on the basis of the sacrifice of Christ. But the divided pieces and the turtle dove and pigeon also prefigure Israel. When Abraham had arranged the sacrifice, "birds of prey came down upon the carcasses, and Abraham drove them away" (v. 11). These birds are evil (cf. Matt. 13:4, 19, 32) and symbolize the predatory nations that would feed upon Israel.

"And when the sun was going down, a deep sleep fell upon Abraham; and, lo, a horror of great darkness fell upon him" (v. 12). It was on the evening following the night during which, in response to his heavenward look, he had received the promise that his descendants should be countless as the stars. The morning hours had been spent in performing the

command to arrange the ceremonial details of the
solemn treaty-making. The afternoon was spent,
doubtless, in a vigil by the side of the divided bodies,
driving away the vultures that came from far and
near, that they might neither pollute nor devour what
had been consecrated to God.

As the sun was setting and the darkness was gathering around Abraham, God's revelation came to His
servant, not in a waking vision as on the previous
night, but in "a deep sleep." Combined with the
heavy slumber was "a horror of great darkness." Both
the "sleep" and the "darkness" were tokens in the
experience of the patriarch of the suffering and affliction coming upon his descendants in the Egyptian
bondage.

While the divine voice announced the four-century-
long servitude of Abraham's posterity in a strange
country, the woeful tidings were relieved by joyful
news of judgment upon the oppressing nation and the
eventual deliverance of God's people "with great sub-
stance" (v. 14). The patriarch himself was promised
a long peaceful life and hope at death, when he would
go to his "fathers in peace" and "be buried in a good
old age" (v. 15).

"And it came to pass, that, when the sun went
down, and it was dark, behold, a smoking furnace,
and a flaming torch that passed between these pieces"
(v. 17). The setting sun, the gathering gloom of
night and the horror of darkness were indications
of the testing not only of God's chosen man of faith,

but precursors of the trials of his posterity and of all those who follow in the steps of his faith.

God was giving an unforgettable demonstration to His ancient friend that the life of faith must frequently be tested by the experience of the waning day, the setting sun and the dark night-gloom that settles all around the man of trust and often falls like a pall upon his soul. But Abraham's gracious Friend was also granting convincing proof of His personal presence with His tested servant and people in their trials, and showing the efficacy of His promises to carry them through dark night experiences to a brighter day.

The Darkness A Preparation for the Dawn

The darkness of the night of trial, indeed, is designed to prepare for the dawning of a new morn, cloudless and glory-filled, dew-bespangled and fresh from the hand of the Creator. The essence of this preparation is the sight of the divine face and a knowledge of the divine love and power, vouch-safed in the night of trial. As the clear peaceful night revealed the multitudinous stars to the patriarch and each shining orb a divine promise of numerous progeny, so the night of "deep sleep" and "horror of darkness," too, brought with it the light of God's immeasurable grace.

The sinking sun and the lengthening shadows of dusk merging into darkness brought with them "a smoking furnace," it is true, but there also appeared "a flaming torch" that passed between the pieces of the slain animals. The "smoking furnace" was a picture of Egypt and the tribulation through which Abraham's descendants through Isaac and Jacob must pass (Deut. 4:20). The "flaming torch," on the other hand, spoke of the light of God's presence with His suffering people in the night of affliction.

The occasion offered a grand display of the truth that, however dark the night through which God's people may be called to pass, the Lord will give the light of His presence and comfort. The "flaming torch" passing between the slain animals was a token not only of God's presence, but of His gracious undertaking and blessing manifested in His ratification of the far-reaching covenant with Abraham centering in the coming Messiah and in the possession of the land of Canaan. "In that day Jehovah made a covenant with Abram, saying, Unto thy seed have I given this land, from the river of Egypt unto the great river, the river Euphrates" (Gen. 15:18).

God's servant was willing to endure trial and testing, and the result was a more intimate acquaintanceship with his divine Friend and far-reaching blessing to himself and to untold generations of others. The representative man of faith lifted his head heavenward and Godward when night came to glimpse not only the stars of twilight but the uncounted millions of stars of night, each one blossoming as a radiant promise of God to his heart.

> *Who never ate his bread in sorrow.*
> *Who never spent the darksome hours*
> *Weeping, and watching for the morrow,*
> *He knows you not, ye heavenly Powers.*
> Johann Wolfgang Goethe

It speaks in thunder from the skies;
    It speaks in rain;
It speaks in slowly breaking hearts;
    It speaks in pain—
The voice that says, no love can come
    Without some loss,
No mystic shining faith can rise
    Without a cross.

Mary Buirgp

STAR COUNTING

He counteth the number of the stars . . . (Psa. 147:4).
. . . Number the stars, if thou be able to number them
. . . (Gen. 15:5).

The upward look in the night of affliction and testing not only brings the sight of the stars but, like God's blessings and promises, innumerable myriads of them. If one examines the clear night sky, with the moon absent, the stars appear countless. Actually, however, only about six thousand of these luminous bodies in the whole heavens are visible *to the unaided eye.* Since only half the sphere is above the horizon at any moment, and since all faint stars are blotted out by near proximity to this planet, the average person with unaided vision can scarcely count more than two thousand stars at any given time.

Stars Visible and Invisible

But because the unaided eye cannot see more than about two thousand stars at any given time is no proof at all that more do not exist. In fact, they do exist in prodigious numbers. Our solar system alone contains immense concentrations of them called galaxies, populated with anywhere from one hundred billion to two hundred billion stars. Even the smallest telescope or opera glass will reveal thousands more stars invisible to the naked eye. Large telescopes penetrate farther and farther into the immensity of space, so that now between one and two billion stars can be sighted and photographed.

What a vast difference between two thousand to six thousand stars visible to the unassisted vision of man and the one to two billion revealed to the human eye through the powerful telescope! What a contrast, too, between what the natural eye sees in the night of trial and what the eye of faith can glimpse when the heavens are dark.

Multitudes "having no hope and without God in the world" (Eph. 2:12) never take the heavenward look when trouble and adversity come, and consequently do not see a single star to relieve the gloom of their night experience. Many children of God, who look skyward when trials overtake them, nevertheless see only with the natural eye, either allowing one small cloud to hide a whole sky full of stars, or glimpsing only a few of God's innumerable lamps of light.

THE TELESCOPE OF FAITH

By contrast the Spirit-directed believer, exercising faith, has his spiritual vision immeasurably increased. His implicit trust in God, especially in times of darkness, acts like a powerful telescope disclosing to him new worlds of divine promises and whole galaxies of revealed truth to illuminate the night and give assurance of God's presence and help.

Abraham's faith acted like such a telescope when God "brought him forth abroad" and directed him to look toward heaven and "number the stars" (Gen. 15:5). It was not the divine intention that the patriarch's vision take in only the comparatively few thousand luminaries which could be seen with the naked eye in the clear Palestinian night heavens. God would have Abraham peer into the distant depths of the illimitable oceans of celestial light and by faith to catch a view of the millions of shining orbs flung out in space.

The patriarch's divine Friend was stimulating his faith and drawing it out into definite action. "Number the stars, if thou be able to number them." The challenge to count the stars was an invitation to His ancient servant to enumerate his blessings, for God was connecting each starry sphere with a divine blessing for Abraham. "So shall thy seed be."

The blessing, however, was not merely in a numerous posterity, but in the faith and the divine calling of these descendants—their spiritual privileges and mission to the world. They were to be "Israelites," whose would be "the adoption, and the glory, and the covenants, and the giving of the law, and the service of God, and the promises" (Rom. 9:4). Most important of all, from them, according to the flesh, would come Christ, the Savior of the world, "who is over all, God blessed for ever" (Rom. 9:5).

It was fitting that a promise which in its far-reaching sweep involved the coming of the world's Redeemer in whom God is most directly glorified, should be set forth in terms of "the heavens" which "declare the glory of God and the firmament" which "showeth his handiwork" (Psa. 19:1). It was suitable, moreover, that such a disclosure, spanning the centuries and focussing in the manifestation of God's glorious salvation, should be illustrated by the vast expanse of the firmament and expounded by the numberless stars.

STAR-COUNTING TIME

The most precious revelations of God and the most wonderful visitations of his love often come during the darkness of a period of personal testing. *Night time is star-counting time!* Each star made visible by the telescope of faith is an added evidence of the goodness of God. Each glistening orb sighted by the Spirit-anointed eye of faith is a token of His tender concern for His children in their experiences of gloom and constitutes another star to count.

> *When upon life's billows you are tempest-tossed,*
> *When you are discouraged, thinking all is lost,*
> *Count your many blessings name them one by one,*
> *And it will surprise you what the Lord hath done.*
>
> *Count your blessings,*
> * Name them one by one;*
> *Count your blessings,*
> * See what God hath done!*
> *Count your blessings,*
> * Name them one by one;*
> *Count your many blessings,*
> * See what God hath done!*
>
> J. Oatman

But who can really count His blessings when, even

in the night of trial, he looks to God *with the eye of faith?* "Look now toward heaven, and number the stars, *if thou be able to number them*" (Gen. 15:5). Faith always opens our spiritual eyes and gives us such a long-range view and telescopic vision that our blessings are multiplied to the point of becoming innumerable. Only unbelief, that hangs a curtain over the sun in the daytime of prosperity and blots out the stars in the night time of adversity, can so diminish our blessings as to make them countable at all, under any circumstances.

Unbelief refuses to see the light in the full noontide glare. No wonder, under the veil of night, it fails to see even the stars visible to the naked eye, and clothes the heavens with unnatural blackness and unrelieved gloom.

But God's man of faith of yesteryear looking skyward with the eye of faith, envisioned vast new worlds of light and Messianic promise.

Our Lord Himself gave intimation of this fact when He said to the unbelieving Jews of His time: "Your father, Abraham, rejoiced to see my day; and he saw it and was glad" (John 8:56). That night many centuries before Christ came, as the patriarch looked at the stars, and was commanded to count them as symbolic of his numerous descendants, he was spanning the years, and with the telescope of faith catching a vision of "the Star out of Jacob" (Num. 24:17).

Envisioning the Coming Messiah and Redeemer, Abraham was foreglimpsing the source of all blessing for a race ruined by sin. He was rejoicing in Him

"who only hath immortality, dwelling in the light unapproachable" (1 Tim. 6:16) and who was to banish
death and bring "life and immortality to light through
the gospel" (2 Tim. 1:10). The patriarch's star-
counting in the dark night of testing in his personal
life, accordingly, comprehended the ultimate blessing
for himself and all men of all time everywhere—the
Coming Savior and Deliverer from sin.

Moreover, night time was star-counting time for
God's ancient man of faith and from the womb of its
darkness were born the most resplendent promises of
hope. And such is the case with God's man of faith
anytime, anywhere. Often out of the pain and anguish
of the night of affliction is brought forth the blessed
child of joyous hope and victory.

Night time was star-counting time for Isaac and
Jacob to whom the promises made to Abraham were
confirmed. The eleven patriarchs, the sons of Jacob,
were seen as stars bowing down to Joseph in his prophetic dream (Gen. 37:9). Moses, in the Wilderness
interceding for Israel in the dark night of their sin
when they had worshipped the golden calf, eloquently
pleads the promises made to the patriarchs: "Remember Abraham, Isaac and Israel, thy servants, to whom
thou swarest by thine own self, and saidst unto them,
I will multiply your seed as the stars of heaven. . ."
(Exod. 32:13). Moses, reviewing God's faithfulness
to His people previous to their entrance into the land
of Canaan could say, "Thy fathers went down into
Egypt with threescore and ten persons; and now Je-

hovah thy God hath made thee as the stars of heaven for multitude" (Deut. 10:22).

HUMAN STAR COUNTERS

Men may and ought to count the stars that God has placed in the firmament to give light in times of darkness. Infinite grace has placed them there as reminders of the promises of God contained in His Word not only to be seen by the eye of faith of the spiritually renewed man, and staggering multitudes of them to be explored by the God-directed man of faith, but the Creator has made some of them so bright and clear that the unaided eye of the natural man may glimpse them and in his night experiences be led to a knowledge of the Creator and the salvation He has provided in Christ.

But star-counting at its best in the spiritual realm with the man of faith is limited, even as it is in the scientific field with the most powerful telescopes in use in modern astronomy. Men of God "through faith" have "subdued kingdoms, wrought righteousness, obtained promises, stopped the mouths of lions, quenched the power of fire, escaped the edge of the sword, from weakness were made strong, waxed mighty in war, turned to flight armies of aliens" (Heb. 11:33, 34). Yet the greatest men of faith who have ever lived have counted but few of God's stars in their night experiences. They have appropriated but a small portion of the vast ocean of God's grace and power opened to them.

Men of science through advanced knowledge have progressively expanded the confines of an illimitable universe, pushing celestial frontiers farther and farther into the depths of fathomless space, discovering new worlds and galaxies of worlds thousand upon thousands of light years away. There are still starry worlds where the most powerful telescopes have not yet penetrated, still billions of luminaries outside the between one-and-two-billion stars that can now be photographed.

When the modern astronomer has done his best with his powerful one-hundred inch Mount Wilson reflector and his eye has swept the night heavens with an incredibly far-reaching gaze, he has still miserably failed to reach the confines of God's created universe or to exhaust the number of God's created orbs of light. After his latest attempts to penetrate the glories of God's celestial firmament, rather than weep, like Alexander the Great of old, that there are no more worlds to conquer, he may more fittingly ponder the words of the inspired psalmist:

O Jehovah, our Lord,
How excellent is thy name in all the earth,
Who has set thy glory upon the heavens!
Out of the mouth of babes and sucklings hast thou estab-
  lished, strength,
Because of thine adversaries,
That thou mightest still the enemy and the avenger.
When I consider thy heavens, the work of thy fingers,
The moon and the stars, which thou hast ordained,
What is man, that thou art mindful of him?
And the son of man, that thou visitest him?
For thou hast made him a little lower than God,
And crownest him with glory and honor.
Thou make'st him to have dominion over the works of thy
  hands;

Thou hast put all things under his feet:
All sheep and oxen,
Yea, and the beasts of the field,
The birds of the heavens, and the fish of the sea,
Whatsoever passeth through the paths of the seas.
O Jehovah, our Lord,
How excellent is thy name in all the earth!

(Psa. 8:1-9).

THE DIVINE STAR COUNTER

Where the creature fails in star-counting, either in the spiritual realm, assisted by the eye of faith, or in the scientific field, aided by the powerful telescope, the Creator of the stars takes over. He who conducted Abraham out under the open heavens and gave His friend a lesson in faith, alone can number the luminaries He has made. That is precisely the reason why the divine instruction to "number the stars" was appended with the illuminating qualification *"if thou be able to number them"* (Gen. 15:5).

The Creator of the starry worlds knew full well, as only He could know, how innumerable were the stellar bodies and how impossible for the creature actually to number them. But He Who had placed them in their spheres to be for "signs" or symbols (Gen. 1:14) was accordingly fully aware of their superlative value as an object lesson in teaching the lessons of faith and illustrating the divine presence and goodness in times of darkness. No wonder God's representative man of faith developed remarkable trust, receiving such teaching from the Master Teacher Himself.

Abraham was not the first nor the last child of

God whose heart has been drawn out in holy awe and in worship upon beholding the glories of the star-studded heavens. A poet in ancient Israel who knew Jehovah as the Builder of Jerusalem, the Gatherer of the outcasts of His people, and in such intimate and vital ways as the Healer of the broken-hearted and wounded, yet exults in praise that such a God of condescending love and gracious ministration is at the same time the omniscient Counter of the stars and the omnipotent Marshaller of the heavenly bodies:

> *Praise ye Jehovah;*
> *For it is good to sing praises to our God,*
> *For it is pleasant, and praise is comely.*
> *Jehovah doth build up Jerusalem.*
> *He gathereth together the outcasts of Israel.*
> *He healeth the broken in heart,*
> *And bindeth up their wounds.*
> *He counteth the number of the stars;*
> *He calleth them all by their names.*
> *Great is our Lord and mighty in power;*
> *His understanding is infinite* (Psa. 147:1-5).

That God counts the number of the stars is a superlative detail of His greatness and power. Men for many millennia have been counting the heavenly bodies but have only barely begun an unfinished and humanly unfinishable task. Only the Creator Himself can count the trillions of stars He has hung out in illimitable space. No one but He knows how many stars are in the sky. No one but He knows, either, how far the sky stretches out in all directions away from the earth. In other words, no one knows how large the universe is except Him Who made it.

As new and more powerful telescopes enable man

to peer farther into outlying space, more and more distant stars are disclosed. Apparently the stars stretch endlessly in all directions. The vast belt of star fields called the Milky Way, a stellar system to which our sun belongs, is bedecked in its lustrous beauty with many billions of luminaries.

With a one-hundred-inch telescope at Mount Wilson, California, objects two hundred and forty million light years away have been photographed. The utter immensity of this space is almost beyond comprehension when we remember that a light year, representing the distance light travels in one year, is six trillion miles. Imagine multiplying six trillion miles by two hundred and forty million to compute the space into which man's eye has pierced.

In this immense celestial ocean, five hundred million galaxies, much like our Milky Way, have been observed. Most of these great stellar clusters contain about the same incalculable numbers of stars as adorn our Milky Way and make it a rim of indescribable splendor.

With new giant telescopes, such as the two-hundred-inch instrument on Mount Palomar, piercing more than twice the distance as the one-hundred-inch device, astronomers will perhaps be able to explore the heavens as far as six quadrillion miles (the unit six with twenty-one ciphers) on all sides of the earth. As this practically infinite expanse of space is fathomed, will men find the stars growing fewer in number? Or as astronomical frontiers are pushed out into the incredible unknown, will it turn out that there are no more stars out there? Only time will furnish the answer, but there is every evidence that other innumerable starry spheres will be discovered, disclosing new evidence of the glory of Him "who counteth the number of the stars."

The Divine Star Namer

God's glory, however, is not only displayed in His counting the number of the stars in the unfathomable expanse of His heavens, but also in His calling them "all by their names." It is a stupendous thought that He should count the innumerable celestial bodies. It is a more staggering declaration that he "calls them *all* by their names" (Psa. 147:4).

From earliest times men have made persistent attempts to name, as well as number, the stars. The starry population of the heavens, however, has been revealed by the modern telescope to be so unbelievably enormous, that human effort is rendered puny in ability to calculate the vast numbers of the stars, much less to name them.

The more luminous stars visible from Europe, perhaps not exceeding two hundred, had special names assigned to them in ancient and medieval times. Some are of Greek origin, but the larger number was named by the Arabs, who carried on the study of astronomy during the Dark Ages. Certain stars are mentioned by name in the Homeric epics as well as in the book of Job. The names of the more striking constellations have survived from antiquity, but have been supplanted by more modern methods of indicating the brighter stars within the constellations by the use of the letters of the Greek and Roman alphabet.

In the eighteenth century the plan of numbering the stars was introduced. This method has since been used, in some form or other, in all catalogs of stars. Whether the catalog embraces the entire heavens or is restricted to certain celestial zones, the stars are commonly numbered in the sense of their increasing right ascension.

Names of some of the specially interesting first magnitude stars include Sirius, Canopus, Vega, Capella, Arcturus, Rigel, Betelgeuse, Pollux and Castor. Other interesting stars include Alphard, Algol, Bellatrix, Cochab, Menkar and Mira.

But star-naming as star-counting on the human level is soon swallowed up in the immensity of space and lost in the bewildering numbers of its starry denizens. When billions upon billions of luminaries crowd in upon the eye of the astronomer as he scans the skies, names become indistinguishable and the task becomes as humanly impossible as counting the sand upon the seashore and naming each particle washed clean and smooth by the ocean's surf.

Star-naming as well as star-counting on the divine level, however, publishes the glory of God. No matter how vast the celestial star fields, no matter how far into illimitable space the stellar meadows may extend, no matter how lavishly carpeted with starry worlds they may be, He knows each one, the brightest as well as the dullest, the largest as well as the smallest, the nearest as well as the farthest away.

He to whom a million light years of celestial space is as an inch, "who hath measured the waters" of the oceans "in the hollow of his hand, and meted out the heavens with the span" (Isa. 40:12) —"*He* counteth the number of the stars, *He* calleth them *all* by their names." The heavens declare His glory, and the firmament shows His handiwork. Because He is God, the mighty Creator, the all-wise Sustainer of the Universe, star-counting and star-naming are just as natural to Him as star-making.

> *Praise ye Jehovah.*
> *Praise ye Jehovah from the heavens:*
> *Praise him in the heights.*
> *Praise ye him, all his angels:*
> *Praise ye him, all his host.*
> *Praise ye him, sun and moon:*
> *Praise him, all ye stars of light.*
> *Praise him, ye heavens of heavens,*
> *And ye waters that are above the heavens*
>   (Psa. 148:1-4).

The starry worlds in far-flung space unceasingly praise the all-powerful and all-wise Creator. Shall man, created with personality and endowed with faculties of perception, fail to do what the inanimate universe constantly does? Surely redeemed man with Spirit-quickened heart and voice attuned to God's grace and goodness, as well as appreciative of His matchless creative skill, must echo the words of another psalmist who sang long ago:

> *Oh give thanks unto Jehovah; for he is good;*
> *For his lovingkindness endureth forever.*
> *Oh give thanks unto the God of gods;*

For his lovingkindness endureth forever.
Oh give thanks unto the Lord of lords;
For his lovingkindness endureth forever:
To him who alone doeth great wonders;
For his lovingkindness endureth forever;
To him that by understanding made the heavens;
For his lovingkindness endureth forever.
To him that spread forth the earth above the waters;
For his lovingkindness endureth forever;
To him that made great lights;
For his lovingkindness endureth forever:
The sun to rule by day;
For his lovingkindness endureth forever
The moon and stars to rule by night;
For his lovingkindness endureth forever

(Psa. 136:1-9).

How thankful man can be that He who "by understanding made the heavens" with "the sun to rule by day" and "the moon and stars to rule by night," and who counteth the vast numbers of celestial luminaries, calling them all by their names, is the God made known to us in covenant mercy as preeminently the One whose "lovingkindness endureth forever."

Lord of all being, throned afar,
Thy glory flames from sun and star;
Center and soul of every sphere,
Yet to each loving heart how near!

Sun of our life, Thy quickening ray
Sheds on our path the glow of day;
Star of our hope, Thy softened light
Cheers the long watches of the night.

Oliver Wendell Holmes

STARLIT PATH THROUGH TRIAL

Chapter Four

Stars of the Twilight

Let the stars of the twilight thereof be dark . . .
(Job 3:9).

EVENING STARS

So we wrought in the work . . . from the rising of the morning till the stars appeared (Neh. 4:21).

Eventide, as light begins to fade and twilight gradually merges into night, is an extraordinarily beautiful part of the day. The splendor of the setting sun, whether as a ball of fire in a cloudless sky or as a magic artist adorning the clouds with unimaginable colors, is but the prelude to the softer, lustre and enchanting loveliness of the gem-bedecked nocturnal heavens.

Before the sun as the monarch of the day has completely surrendered his rule and retired for a brief night season, and while yet his fading glory guilds the sky, the evening stars appear. Silently, one by one, they begin to blossom in the celestial meadows like fields of flowers. First the brightest of them shines forth, followed by the less luminous.

Evening stars are any of the bright planets seen in the west at the close of day. Sometimes the luminary is Venus shining with a clear dazzling brilliance, sometimes Jupiter and, at other seasons, Mercury. Thus, actually the stars that are most brilliant and accordingly appear first in the evening sky after sunset are not stars at all, but planets. Unlike stars, which are huge spheres of incandescent gas like our sun, the planets are much smaller than most stars, have no light nor heat of their own, but, mirror-like, simply reflect the light of the sun. While countless trillions of stars stud the farthest expanses of the heavens, only nine planets are known, and all belong to our solar system.

On a clear evening, as the sun sets and the afterglow of the western sky fades, the planets Venus, Jupiter, or Mercury, according to their changing position in the various seasons of the year, are first glimpsed because of their superior radiance. Then as twilight deepens, these celestial "wanderers" (the word "planet" means a "wanderer") become framed in a thicker and thicker background of fixed stars. Planets do not ordinarily twinkle like stars, but shine with a steady, unwavering light, as they move on endlessly in their courses. As evening advances and night sets in, they merge their lustrous beauty with the splendor of the multitudinous twinkling stars, and signal the time for man's rest after the toil of the day.

THE RISING OF THE MORNING

As the stars of the evening betoken the approach of rest-time for work-weary man, so the dawning of the morning signifies the beginning of his labor, after the refreshment of a night's sleep.

The glory of a new day with the sun flooding the earth with light, and adorning each drop of cooling dew with golden radiance, awakens man to new tasks and new achievements. All the weariness of yesterday's toil is forgotten and the ascending dawn, welcomed by the singing of birds and the hum of activity in the animal world, issues a call to work and summons refreshed workers to renewed endeavors.

The rebuilding of the walls of Jerusalem in the days of Nehemiah presents an instructive picture of arduous work for God undertaken early in the morning and assiduously continued against all odds and opposition till dark. "So we wrought in the work . . . from the rising of the morning till the stars appeared" (Neh. 4:21). The Hebrew original is graphic. "So we carried on the task . . . from the ascent of the dawn till the stars came out."

What a scene of concerted diligent service for God! As the first streaks of dawn are illuminating the eastern sky, the people of Jerusalem, each assigned a specific part of the wall, are wending their way through the morning chill and the shadows of the low places to the place of work assigned them.

Each one invigorated by the keen morning air, and fired by love for God and God's city, sets himself resolutely to the difficult task. As "the sun rose upon" Jacob "as he passed over Penuel" limping upon his thigh after his historic night-long struggle with God at the ford of the Jabbok (Gen. 32:31), so the dawning day rose upon the people of Jerusalem as they worked and struggled against desperate odds to restore the city walls.

The sun of God's favor always rises upon the Lord's people whenever they set themselves to do His will and perform those "good works" unto which they have been saved, and which He has "afore prepared" that they "should walk in them" (Eph. 2:10). After the night of struggle, as in the case of Jacob, or after the night of relaxing sleep, the rising of the morning should find every believer, as Nehemiah's wall repairers, at his post of witness and service for God. Being found there, the sun of God's favor will rise upon him and illuminate and bless his path all the day.

THE DIFFICULTIES OF THE DAY

Being found at God's post at the rising of the morning is exceedingly important. It assures us a good start and blessing in the work of God throughout the day. But it does not shield us from the difficulties of the day, nor the heat and burden of noontide. The will of God does not grant exemption from trial and temptations. It rather guarantees that such testings will come and that we should be prepared to meet them.

Am I a soldier of the cross—
A follower of the Lamb?
And shall I fear to own His cause,
Or blush to speak His name?

Must I be carried to the skies
On flowery beds of ease,
While others fought to win the prize,
And sailed through bloody seas?

Are there no foes for me to face?
Must I not stem the flood?
Is this vile world a friend to grace,
To help me on to God?

Since I must fight if I would reign,
Increase my courage, Lord;
I'll bear the toil, endure the pain
Supported by Thy Word!

Nehemiah and his corps of willing workers began

their noble work at the dawning of the day with the rising sun shining auspiciously upon them. But soon their consecrated efforts were to be challenged by all sorts of trials and discouragements.

Sanballat, an influential leader in hostile Samaria, resolutely opposed the refortification of Jerusalem and did everything in his power to halt Nehemiah's work. He was thoroughly "grieved" to think that someone had come on the scene "to seek the welfare of the children of Israel" (Neh. 2:10). Assisted by another unscrupulous person, Tobiah, the Ammonite, false accusation was first resorted to. He and Tobiah suggested to the Persian king that Nehemiah was plotting revolt (Neh. 2:19).

Failing in this device, Sanballat and his henchmen tried derision. Addressing his colleagues and the army of Samaria, "he mocked the Jews" and jeeringly taunted: "What are these feeble Jews doing? Will they fortify themselves? Will they sacrifice? Will they make an end in a day? Will they revive the stones out of the heaps of rubbish, seeing they are burned?" (Neh. 4:2).

Tobiah the Ammonite also laughed to scorn the work being done at Jerusalem. "Even that which they are building, if a fox go up, he shall break down their stone wall" (Neh. 4:3).

Ridicule of this sort is a mighty weapon. Many strong men of faith have fallen under it. Many who can stand up under direct attacks and valiantly face open opposition, wither under the lash of sarcasm. Many can endure anything but to be laughed at. The

titter of the derider has been more damaging to many
of God's servants than the flash of cold steel and
the tumult of direct battle assault.

But Nehemiah and the people of Jerusalem had a
heart to pray and "a mind to work" (Neh. 4:6). Accordingly, they were not to be turned aside from important business for God by the scoffing jeers of their
enemies. They prayed and kept busy in a noble endeavor and derision lost its power to affect them.

Their enemies, however, were not to give up so
easily. Mockery failing, they tried violence and direct
attack. Sanballat and Tobiah gathered others around
them—Arabians, Ammonites and Ashdodites—in a
conspiracy to use force. Behind them was the enemy
of God and God's people, Satan, who always seeks to
hinder the work of God. His work of opposition is
the same in every age. If he cannot discourage the
Lord's people by derisive sneers, he brings direct attack upon them.

In this very crucial time in the rebuilding of the
walls, Satan's work was not entirely unsuccessful. In
the face of such serious testing, discouragement developed among some of God's people and from a
quarter least suspected. Judah, the princely tribe, whose
emblem was the lion, began to become timid and
fainthearted. Their defeatism became vocal. "The
strength of the bearer of burdens is decayed" wailed
Judah, "and there is much rubbish, so that we are
not able to build the wall" (Neh. 4:10).

PRAYER-WARRIORS AND SPEAR-HOLDERS
One of the most remarkable characteristics of

Nehemiah's leadership in the work of God was his spontaneous prayer. This was his basic resource and the secret of his success. By prayer he overcame every attack of the enemy, whether ridicule, discouragement or attack. When the difficulties of the work threatened to overwhelm him, recourse to prayer was as natural to him as showers and flowers are to springtime.

When the people of God were being maligned and scorned, Nehemiah cried: "Hear, O our God, for we are despised: and turn back their reproach upon their own head, and give them up for a spoil in a land of captivity and cover not their iniquity, and let not their sin be blotted out from before thee; for they have provoked thee to anger before the builders" (Neh. 4:4, 5).

When the enemy determined upon violence, Nehemiah said: "We made our prayer unto our God" (Neh. 4:9). Prayer was their first line of defense. Dependence upon divine help was humbly acknowledged. The next thing they did was to take every precaution against the enemy. "We made our prayer unto God, and set a watch against them day and night, because of them" (Neh. 4:9). They committed their case to God, but they did not tempt God. They mixed practical common sense with faith and acted with piety as well as with wisdom. They realized that God would do what they could not do, but He was at the same time expecting them to do what they could do. Faith is never presumption.

Moreover, they not only prayed and trusted God. They were prepared to fight as well. Nehemiah, acting in the energy of faith, knew that God was on their side and would battle for them. With this conviction he prepared the people for the threatened conflict, arming them with swords, spears and bows. They were not only to fight a winning battle in prayer on the spiritual plane (Eph. 6:10-20), but ward off any attack on the natural plane.

Nehemiah after ordering the people to be accoutered for conflict, addressed them with inspiring words: "Be ye not afraid of them: remember the Lord, who is great and terrible, and fight for your brethren, your sons, and your daughters, your wives, and your houses" (Neh. 4:14).

It was a crucial moment. Everything was at stake. A wicked and relentless enemy could be expected to show no mercy. The blessed battle cry was raised aloft: "Remember the Lord!" Remembering Him Who had dealt so graciously with His people, there could be no defeat. Prayer-warriors and spear-holders were to be invincible.

With the conflict won both on the spiritual and on the natural plane, God's work could proceed to completion. "And it came to pass, when our enemies heard that it was known unto us, and God had brought their counsel to nought, that we returned all of us to the wall, everyone unto his work" (Neh. 4:15). Only thus as the servants of God conquer in prayer and through faith can true service for God proceed unimpeded and brought to full fruition.

Till the Stars Appeared

Having confounded their enemies and having resumed work on the wall, Nehemiah and his workers did not become careless. No one who labors for God and achieves for His glory can afford to become unwary. "Be sober, be watchful; your adversary the devil, as a roaring lion, walketh about, seeking whom he may devour: whom withstand stedfast in your faith . . ". (I Peter 5:8, 9). Never does the servant of the Lord know when or where the enemy may strike. Always he must be on the lookout.

Nehemiah and the people continued to be on their guard. Half of his servants "wrought in the work, and half of them held the spears, and shields, and the bows, and the coats of mail . . . everyone with one of his hands wrought in the work, and with the other held his weapon; and the builders everyone had his sword by his side, and so builded" (Neh. 4:16-18).

A trumpeter was stationed at Nehemiah's side. If he sounded an alarm that there was danger, the workers were to gather together, assured that "our God will fight for us."

"So we wrought in the work: and half of them held the spears from the rising of the morning *till the stars appeared*" (Neh. 4:21). It was a long and gruelling work day, from dawn till dusk. As the sun sank behind the western horizon, and as the evening stars, the luminous planets, first were seen, followed soon after by multitudinous fixed stars, the weary people at the signal of these harbingers of night and rest, wended their way home.

Tired and completely exhausted physically, yet spiritually the people were strengthened by the joyous satisfaction of having labored for God and for

God's city. The sweet consciousness that something attempted for God and something done had earned a night's repose, must have filled the heart of each willing worker, as he lay upon his bed and looked out of his window at the stars shining down upon his beloved city.

How shall it be with our service? Do we labor for God "from the rising of the morning . . . till the stars appear?" Shall we receive His approbation at the judgment seat of Christ: "Well done, good and faithful servant, enter into the joy of thy Lord?"

> *Shall I empty handed be*
> *When beside the crystal sea*
> *I shall stand before the everlasting throne?*
> *Must I have a heart of shame*
> *As I answer to my name,*
> *With no works that my Redeemer there can own?*
>
> *If my gratitude I'd show*
> *Unto Him who loves me so,*
> *Let me labor till the evening shadows fall;*
> *That some little gift of love*
> *I may bear to realms above,*
> *And not empty-handed be when comes the call.*
>
> *When the harvest days are past,*
> *Shall I hear Him say at last*
> *"Welcome, toiler, I've prepared for thee a place?"*
> *Shall I bring Him golden sheaves,*
> *Ripened fruit, not faded leaves,*
> *When I see the blessed Savior face to face?*
>   N. A. McAulay
>   Maud Frazer

DUSK AND DARKENED STARS

Remember also thy Creator in the days of thy youth . . .
before the stars are darkened, and the clouds return after
the rain (Eccl. 12:1, 2).

The stars can be darkened! Although no tempest cloud may obscure their lustre and the nocturnal heavens may be perfectly clear, the heavenly luminaries may withdraw their light and become invisible to men. This is true both physically and spiritually.

Job describes the infinite Creator of the celestial spheres as one who controls the heavenly bodies and shuts up or "seals the stars" so that they cannot shine:

> *That commandeth the sun, and it riseth not,*
> *And sealeth up the stars;*
> *That alone stretcheth out the heavens,*
> *And treadeth upon the waves of the sea;*
> *That maketh the Bear, Orion and the Pleiades,*
> *And the chambers of the south* (Job 9:7-9).

There is coming the great and terrible "day of the Lord," climaxed by the second advent of the Messiah, when the heavens shall "tremble" and "the sun and the moon" shall be "darkened," and "the stars withdraw their shining" (Joel 2:10). This great apocalyptic period will be characterized by vast celestial commotions with "signs in the sun and moon and stars; and upon the earth distress of nations . . . for the powers of the heavens shall be shaken" (Luke 21:25).

But the stars may be darkened in a spiritual sense also. Unbelief in the dark night of adversity may so blind our spiritual vision that the brightest stars of

God's gracious care are darkened, if not blotted out altogether.

OLD AGE AND DARKENED STARS

The ancient inspired Hebrew poet-philosopher describes godless maturity and old age as "the evil days" that follow the period of youth, in which God has been neglected and the Creator forgotten (Eccl. 12:1). To him they are the wearisome years that "draw nigh," when the person who has not responded to the clear call of God and the tender overtures of divine grace in youth, becomes self-centered and calloused in heart concerning spiritual things, and sadly confesses, "I have no pleasure in them."

To the ancient sage, godless old age is the time of life when "the sun and the light, and the moon, and the stars, are darkened, and the clouds return after the rain" (Eccl. 12:2). The sun and the light belong to the day. The moon, and the stars relate to the night. But whether in the day of prosperity or in the night of adversity, "the lights," which God caused to shine "in the firmament of heaven" and which He placed there as "signs" or visible symbols of His creatorship and goodness (Gen. 1:14) and of "his everlasting power and divinity" (Rom. 1:20), become darkened and meaningless in their deeper spiritual significance to a mind that in youth has consistently crowded God out of its thinking.

The sun speaks of Christ "the sun of righteousness" who will at His second advent "arise with healing in his beams" (Mal. 4:2 margin), "and who is a "sun and shield" (Psa. 84:11) to His people. The moon symbolizes the church, which reflects the light of Christ in this dark world of sin, as the moon reflects the light of the sun (Gen. 1:16). The stars represent individual believers who shine as "lights in the world, holding forth the word of life" (Phil. 2:15, 16). But to the mind that has never opened to the grace of God in the impressionable years of childhood and youth, and has gone on in unbelief and rejection of God into adulthood, middle life and the cynicism of old age, such great verities have no more reality than would a sun, moon or star giving forth no light.

Such a God-rejecting mind is not only like day with darkened sun and night with eclipsed moon and bedimmed stars, but also like the storm "when the clouds return after the rain." Instead of clear skies and warm reviving sun gilding with gold a well-watered earth and caressing it into radiant fruitfulness, chill drenching rains recur to flood the soil, rot seed and fruit, and afflict man with physical distempers and temporal woes.

Godless old age is like a fruit that never ripens, and remains green and sour, instead of sun-kissed with golden color and mellowed into delicious ripeness. It is like a beautiful flower that never opens, but is stricken by drought and destroyed by insects and disease. It is like a noble tree that is cursed with blight and as a monument of death lifts bare leafless branches bleached by sun and wind.

God's ancient philosopher gives a graphic portrayal of the physical incapacities and the miseries of old age, particularly as those natural sufferings are accentuated by the absence of a knowledge of God in the life. He describes that time as "the day when the keepers of the house (the arms?) shall tremble, and the strong men (the limbs?) shall bow themselves, and the grinders (the teeth?) shall cease because they are few, and those that look out of the windows (the eyes?) shall be darkened and the doors (the ears?) shall be shut in the street; when the sound of the grinding (hearing?) is low, and one shall rise up at the voice of a bird (insomnia?) and all the daughters of music (natural delights?) shall be brought low . . . and desires shall fail" (Eccl. 12:3-5).

Death is described as the "silver cord" being "loosed" and the "golden bowl broken" and "the pitcher . . . broken at the fountain." "And the dust returneth to the earth as it was, and the spirit returneth unto God who gave it" (Eccl. 12:6, 7).

YOUTH AND STAR-STUDDED SKIES

Whereas the sky of godless old age is starless or, at best filled with darkened stars, the sky of buoyant God-responsive youth is studded with meadows of resplendent luminaries. Romantic, imaginative youth not only sees the stars that are there, but often those that are not, as it boldly builds its air-castles and hitches its wagon to stars that exist only in youth's fantasyland.

Although only a dreamland, youth's fantasyland is a delightful realm, nevertheless. In fact, it is an illimitable empire all its own in which the irrepressible enthusiasms and exhaustless energies of youth may soar and be unbounded by time or space or the humdrum happenings of a workaday world.

The growing youngster has difficulty imagining a pot of gold set at the end of the rainbow or envisioning a Santa Claus in a toy-packed reindeer-drawn sleigh skimming through the frosty December air at Christmas time. Youth counts the diamond on the dew-bespangled grass and peoples woodland and meadow with frolicking sprites and dancing elves.

But youth's world is not merely a world of imaginative dreams. It is a world of solid reality as well. It has marvelous discernment of truth as well as beautiful faith to appropriate it. With misty eyes it listens to the great stories of God's Word. It is stirred with rapturous delight by the Christmas story and with the shepherds worships the Christ Child in the Bethlehem manger and with the wise men follows the gleaming star to bow before the Savior of the world.

The ancient inspired philosopher had a fine realization that youth is the period of keen moral, intellectual and spiritual sensitivity. He calls it "the dawn of life" (Eccl. 11:10) and thereby likens its fresh vigor and uncalloused impressionableness to the birth of a new day, when nature awakens with the singing of the birds, and every plant and flower opens expectantly to greet the rising sun. To him it is the joyous, carefree, spontaneously responsive time of life, when the entire personality is alert to the world about, the supernatural as well as the natural.

Aware that the whole physical, mental, emotional and spiritual being of youth is keyed to boundless vitality, God's ancient sage challenges young people of every age with a timeless appeal. "Remember also thy

Creator in the days of thy youth, before the evil days come, and the years draw nigh, when thou shalt say, I have no pleasure in them" (Eccl. 12:1).

In contrast to "the evil days" of godless old age, the writer of Ecclesiastes sees youth as the "good" time of life when all the powers of body, soul and spirit are most keenly active and at their best. The body is the strongest and ought to be given to Him who created it (Psa. 100:3) and redeemed it and to whom it belongs (1 Cor. 6:19, 20). The soul is most sensitive to the movings of God's Spirit in youth and ought then to accept the gift of salvation. The mind is then most active and ought "to remember" its Creator and serve Him faithfully.

The Old Testament sage aptly characterizes God-responsive youth as the period *"before* the sun, and the light, and the moon, and the stars are darkened" (Eccl. 12:2). This is the poet-philosopher's way of graphically setting forth youth's sensitivity to God the Creator's call and claims upon the life. It is his unique way of describing the spontaneous response of the young to what the Apostle Paul in the New Testament calls "Whatsoever things are true, whatsoever things are honorable, whatsoever things are just, whatsoever things are pure, whatsoever things are lovely, whatsoever things are of good report" (Phil. 4:8).

Since "whatsoever things are true . . . honorable . . . just . . . pure . . . lovely and of good report" find their source and center in the revelation of God in Christ, the undarkened sun and light by day and the undimmed moon and stars by night speak of the full knowledge of God's love and grace, and full response in appropriating faith. This, in Old Testament terminology, is to "remember . . . thy Creator."

To remember one's Creator in youth is to remember Him at the right time. It is the proper time because the soul is then unhardened by repeated acts of unbelief and unresponsiveness in the face of the normal responsiveness of youth.

It is thus faith in God that orientates the irresistable energies and properly channels the boundless enthusiasms of youth. Faith brings an undimmed sun and unobscured light to youth in the day of prosperity. It brings an unobscured moon and star-studded skies in the night of adversity.

Faith in God will make the soul of youth respond to the beautiful and good, and call forth every virtue and godly impulse. The sunset will be more magnificent, the thunderous cataract more awesome, the snow-capped mountain peak more majestic and the quiet brook meandering through flowered meadow more charming to the soul that has found its peace in God and sees Him manifested, not only in Christ, but in the manifold beauties of His creation.

> *All the world seemed to sing*
> *Of the Savior and King*
> *When peace sweetly came to my heart.*
> *Troubles all fled away*
> *And my night turned to day,*
> *Blessed Jesus, how glorious thou art!*

How many, who have never felt the touch of God upon their soul, are like "Peter Bell" in William Wordsworth's well-known poem by that name:

> *He roved among the vales and streams,*
>   *In greenwood and the hollow dell.*
> *They were his dwellings night and day—*
> *But nature ne'er could find the way*
>   *Into the heart of Peter Bell . . . .*

Wordsworth's own response reminds us of the undarkened sun and star-studded sky of the youth of yesteryear who remembered the Creator in the dawn of life, referred to by the writer of the book of Ecclesiastes:

> *My heart leaps up when I behold*
>   *A rainbow in the sky:*
> *So was it when my life began:*
> *So is it now I am a man,*
> *So be it when I shall grow old,*
>   *Or let me die!*

Wordsworth's exquisite sentiments in his immortal "I Wandered Lonely as a Cloud" even more graphically give us an insight into a God-touched soul keenly alive to all the beauty of God's creation:

> *I wandered lonely as a cloud*
> *That floats on high o'er vale and hills,*
> *When all at once I saw a crowd,*
> *A host of golden daffodils;*
> *Beside the lake, beneath the trees,*
> *Fluttering and dancing in the breeze.*
>
> *Continuous as the stars that shine*
> *And twinkle on the Milky Way,*
> *They stretch in never-ending line*
> *Along the margin of a bay:*
> *Ten thousand saw I at a glance,*
> *Tossing their heads in sprightly dance.*

The waves beside them danced, but they
Outdid the sparkling waves in glee:—
A poet could not but be gay
In such a jocund company;
I gazed—and gazed—but little thought
What wealth the show to me had brought.

For oft, when on my couch I lie
In vacant or in pensive mood,
They flash upon the inner eye
Which is the bliss of solitude,
And then my heart with pleasure fills,
And dances with the daffodils.

Tested Saint and Darkened Stars

No matter how dark the night of suffering or affliction that may descend upon the child of God, and no matter how the stars of God's gracious love may, under the pressure of trial and momentary flagging faith, seem to become invisible and fade into the deepening dusk, they are never actually darkened. Like God's unchanging love for His tested child, they shine just as radiantly and lustrously in adversity as in prosperity. All that is needed to see them is the unshakable conviction, acting like a telescope, that refuses to doubt the glorious fact of God's faithfulness:

My son, regard not lightly the chastening of the Lord,
Nor faint when thou art reproved of him.
For whom the Lord loveth he chasteneth,
And scourgeth every son whom he receiveth.

(Heb. 12: 5, 6)

To realize that God sometimes allows afflictions, poverty, bereavement, sickness and other calamities to come upon His own in order to refine their character, turn them from their own will to His blessed way, to hide pride in them, and to draw them closer to Himself, is to possess the telescope of faith that enables the tried saint to glimpse the stars, clear and bright, in the dark night of trial.

God's ancient servant Job wrestled with this age-old problem why the righteous suffer. In discovering the reason, he found the answer not only for himself, but for all the people of God everywhere and in every age.

Job was rich. In fact he was the richest man in the East in his day. He had large property holdings of cattle and real estate. A fine home, a large family, prosperity and health were his. In addition, he was godly. He was "perfect and upright" and "feared God and turned away from evil" (Job 1:1). This does not mean that God's saint was in any sense sinless, as the whole purpose of his trials shows, but simply that he was wholly on God's side and very pious.

But Job, like many of God's own, needed spiritual refinement which only the furnace-experience of suffering could bring about. To effect this gracious purpose, God permits Satan to touch His servant. Property and family are swept away. Next Job is afflicted with loathsome boils, apparently the horrible black leprosy of Egypt. He is reduced to the ash heap outside an Oriental village, where he alleviates his terrible misery by scraping his itching sores with a piece of broken pottery.

To add to his misery his wife urges him to renounce God and die, and thus end his suffering. To crown his wretchedness, he loses his good name among his friends, who came to comfort him, but by their erroneous explanation of his sufferings as caused by gross personal sin, rather discomfort him.

God's servant is a sad spectacle, as he is thus abysmally reduced to the depths of despair. But he demonstrates himself as God's own and in line for God's purifying and chastening ministry by refusing to renounce the Lord.

Moreover, Job in the midnight hour of his life, gives prompt evidence of his need for spiritual refinement. In a spirit that is far from humble or submissive he begins deliriously to curse the day in which he was born:

> *Let the day perish wherein I was born,*
> *And the night which said,*
> *There is a man child conceived.*
> *Let that day be darkness;*
> *Let not God from above seek for it,*
> *Neither let the light shine upon it.*
> *Let darkness and the shadow of death claim it for their own;*
> *Let a cloud dwell upon it.*
> *Let all that maketh black the day terrify it* (Job 3:3-5).

Job also wildly curses the night in which he was conceived and desires it be blotted from the calendar:

> *As for that night let thick darkness seize upon it:*
> *Let it not rejoice among the days of the year;*
> *Let it not come into the number of the months* (Job 3:6).

And then the overwrought saint does a strange thing. Instead of seeing the stars of God's gracious love in his midnight experience, he curses with darkness the morning stars because they, as the brightest of the celestial luminaries, are the harbingers of the dawning of a new day, that would blot out the darkness of the night in which he was conceived:

> Let the stars of the twilight thereof be dark;
> Let it look for light, but have none;
> Neither let it behold the eyelids of the morning:
> Because it shut not up the doors of my mother's womb,
> Nor hid trouble from mine eyes (Job 3:9, 10).

Such reckless bitterness over the calamity that had befallen him can scarcely be consonant with a calm faith that has the unswerving conviction "that to them that love God all things work together for good, even to them that are called according to his purpose" (Rom. 8:28). The man who thus curses the night of his conception or birth so vehemently that he would blot out the most lustrous stars that twinkle through the twilight of dawn and announce the ending of its darkness and the breaking of a new day, thereby displays his desperate need for humility, self-abnegation and submission to the divine will. The man who would not permit the dusk of that fateful night to be dissipated by the dawn raising its eyelids and with the first rays of morning projecting its light into a new day, is a real subject for the tender refining touch of a God of infinite love.

But God's grace triumphs. Job's three friends present false accusations and wrong diagnoses of his case, yet as a result of their clumsy probings, Job's self-righteousness and pride are revealed. Thereupon Elihu berates God's servant because he justifies himself rather than God (Job 34:1-37) and in a beautiful way states what is God's purpose in permitting the righteous to suffer:

> *That he may withdraw man from his purpose,*
> *And hide pride from man* (Job 33:17).

Not until the Lord Himself with dramatic sweep and in a burst of glory speaks to Job out of the whirlwind is God's servant humbled and made to see his self-righteousness and pride. Then the tried saint perceives the refining purpose of his suffering and utters the climactic words that mark his spiritual renovation:

> *I had heard of thee by the hearing of the ear,*
> *But now mine eye seeth thee;*
> *Wherefore I abhor myself*
> *And repent in dust and ashes* (Job 42:5. 6).

What a complete transformation from the bitter and unsubmissive spirit that cursed the night of his conception, deliriously pronouncing eternal darkness upon it as he had cried out, "Let the stars of the twilight thereof be dark."

Divine grace, however, was not to darken any stars in Job's sky, but rather in its marvelous outworking, to bring out a whole new sky full of them, brighter and more glorious than the morning stars God's harassed saint had wanted to curse.

When the Lord had tried his ancient servant and proved him, then He was ready to restore him again to favor and blessing. Accordingly, Job is reinstated to double his former prosperity and happiness. He had been tested in the furnace of divine love. In the process he had seen the dross—his pride and self-righteousness —consumed and the gold refined. Would that we, like Job, may be able to say when periods of testing come in our experience, as in his:

But he knoweth the way I take,
When he hath tried me, I shall come forth a's gold
                                        (Job 23:10).

Does Jesus care when my heart is pained
        Too deeply for mirth or song;
                As the burdens press
                And the cares distress,
And the way grows weary and long?

Does Jesus care when my way is dark
        With a nameless dread and fear?
                As the daylight fades
                Into deep night shades,
Does He care enough to be near?

O yes, He cares.
I know He cares,
His heart is touched with my grief;
        When the days are weary,
        The long nights dreary,
I know my Savior cares.
                                Frank E. Graeff.

STARLIT PATH THROUGH TROUBLE

Chapter Five

Tempest and Starless Night

. . . I will cover the heavens, and make the stars thereof dark . . . (Ezek. 32:7).

STORMS AND STARS

And, when neither sun nor stars shone upon us for many days, and no small tempest lay on us, all hope that we should be saved was now taken away (Acts 27:20).

A storm is frequently a destructive and fearful thing, taking a heavy toll in life and property. The tropical hurricane, like some huge Titan run amuck, can churn the sea into a wild seething maelstrom and lay waste vast sections of the countryside. The dreaded cyclone, although much more localized in its extent than the hurricane, is even more deadly in its terrifying fury as it twists and smashes everything in its path. High winds, torrential rains, heavy hail and lightning of the ordinary storm often cause widespread damage. Severe snowstorms, too, can occasion great suffering and loss of property and life.

Storms undeniably have a destructive aspect. But both in the physical and spiritual realm they are intended to be a blessing in disguise. The mighty hurricane may toss a ship like a feather upon the raging ocean, but it brings the occupants to realize their own helplessness and the power of God. Its destructive force may run rough shod over large sections of country, uprooting trees and destroying homes. But it brings copious rains that revive drought-ridden fields and scorched meadows.

The reckless tornado may strike in an instant,

decimating one's home and perhaps taking away loved ones. But it brings with it the incalculably valuable lesson that "a man's life consisteth not in the abundance of things which he possesseth" (Luke 12:15). The dark tempest may blot out the sun and stars, but it brings with it the light and face of God.

The swirling blizzard may make the countryside impassable for days and reduce the humming metropolis to silent inactivity. But it bedecks bush and branch, tree and shrub with an exquisite jewelled mantle of fleecy white and covers the commonest object and the most squalid hovel with a robe of celestial purity.

STORMS AND GOD'S WILL

It is commonly supposed that storms come only to those who are ungodly or to those who disobey God's commands. This is, of course, far from the case. There is most emphatically the tempest that overtakes a sinner as a just penalty for his sin or that engulfs one of God's own, like Jonah of old, who runs away from God's call. But storms may also come in the pathway of obedience to the divine will.

The storm on the Galilean lake into which the disciples of our Lord ran is a case in point. The tempest was not the result of the disciples' following their own way, but in following Christ's way. Matthew distinctly tells us Jesus did the leading and the disciples the following when they ran into the Tiberian tempest. "And when he was entered into a boat, his disciples followed him. And, behold, there arose a great tempest in the sea, insomuch that the boat was covered with waves" (Matt. 8:23, 24) .

Not only did the disciples run into a storm while following the Lord, but "a great tempest." The little boat in which they were riding was being tossed mercilessly by the waves and rapidly beginning to fill with water. It was a desperate crisis. The situation appeared utterly hopeless. Death in a watery grave seemed to be an imminent doom.

To the believer, walking in the will of God, the world is a Tiberian lake, sometimes calm and beautiful, but quickly angered and frequently unmanageably boisterous. When the disciples set out with Jesus to cross the lake, it was evening (Mark 4:35) . The sun was declining in the western sky. Day ended peacefully in a burst of glory and the surface of the water was as smooth as glass when night lowered a soft curtain around them, spangled with numberless stars.

Soon, however, a wind came up and dark clouds blotted out the stars. A violent storm was raging. Feverishly the disciples rowed and toiled to keep the ship afloat. In their consternation they saw that human efforts were unavailing. The harder they worked, the more hopeless their position became. They were transfixed with fear. It was then that they were indeed in a tragic plight.

Although the Christian's pilgrimage through the world is beset by storms without, only those that develop within are really dangerous. Only when the disciples allowed the tempest to invade their own hearts, did they lose the sense of assurance and fearlessness that comes from a knowledge of being in the will of God and possessing the presence and help of God.

Only when the disciples forgot that Jesus, although "asleep" in the stern on a pillow, was in the boat with them, did the storm get into their hearts, causing them to be paralyzed by fear and to forfeit self-control. Losing the sense of the Lord's presence, they became harassed and severely strained. Then unbelief became vocal in a torrent of impatience and harsh criticism: "Teacher, carest thou not that we perish?" (Mark 4:38).

Imagine even in their fear and nervous irritation accusing Him of a lack of concern for them, after all the proofs of His love that had been vouchsafed to them on numerous occasions. It was plain they needed the lessons that only the storm could bring, and He, who was with them in the boat, was using this tempest to instruct them.

It is a consolation to know whatever commotions may lie in the way of Christian obedience, they are designed for some good purpose. Storms that come in the performance of God's will are never an accident. They are carefully appointed and timed for the child of God by divine wisdom and are for some good purpose.

In the case of the disciples and experience of lashing waves and howling winds showed them their sinfulness and helplessness. More than that, the dire extremity to which they were reduced revealed to them the wonderful graciousness and power of Him Whom they had with them in the boat. The most blessed result of all, perhaps, was that in their trouble the disciples began to enquire after the Lord. The experience of peril developed in them a holy desire to know Christ. Not until the fury of the waves had subsided at His omnipotent "Peace, be still" and the "wind ceased, and there was a great calm" did the supremely important question come from their hearts and lips: *"Who then is* this?" (Mark 4:39, 40).

This is the ultimate benefit the storm is designed to bestow upon us—a desire *to know Christ*. There is no finer quest in all the world than to seek Him, no more exalted wisdom than to know Him. The life motto of the Apostle Paul is still the noblest that any Christian can possibly choose: "That I may know him, and the power of his resurrection, and the fellowship of his sufferings, being conformed unto his death" (Phil. 3:10). O blessed storm that brings us to a deeper knowledge of the Son of God!

STORMS AND STARLESS NIGHT

All storms, of course, are not of the same duration of time or intensity. Some may be no more than a fleeting summer shower. Others may be brief, but violent. Brewed in the intense heat of midsummer, they burst forth with sudden violence, cover the parched ground with hail, deluge it with rain and bring with it cool refreshment. Others are accompanied by phenomenal pyrotechnical displays of flashing lightning, deep peals of reverberating thunder, and raging flood waters that cause vast destruction to life and property. Winter storms frequently bury the landscape in a snowy grave or load it under millions of tons of ice, that produce a fairyland of beauty, but break to pieces the mightiest oaks of the forest.

God's storms also vary in length and severity and are adapted to the spiritual seasons of our experience. Often the Father's love can accomplish His all-wise and beneficent purpose simply by the cloudy day and the softly falling shower gently refreshing furrow and field for springtime fruitfulness. Again the lightning flash of His wrath, and the thunderous roll of His judgments are necessary.

Often there must be the protracted fury of the blast and the decimating power of raging flood waters pulling down and destroying preparatory to building up and restoring. Frequently God's working in the stormy experience in our lives is like His commission to Jeremiah, two-thirds of which was destructive. "See I have this day set thee over the nations and over the kingdoms, to pluck up and to break down and to destroy and to overthrow, to build and to plant" (Jer. 1:10).

The storm into which Jonah ran as he was fleeing from God's will was to a large extent aimed at disciplining the self-willed and selfish prophet. The terrible experience in the briny deep and in the fish's stomach purged God's servant and made him ready and willing to go to Nineveh on his preaching mission.

The longest and most furious storm recorded in the Bible is that sunless and starless experience of the Apostle Paul when he suffered shipwreck on his way to Rome. For two full weeks the vessel, on which he was a passenger, was violently tossed to and fro in the Adriatic Sea between Crete and the island of Melita (Malta).

The ordeal must have been indeed a trying one for the Apostle, especially when he had warned the centurion, under whose authority he was being taken to Rome as a prisoner, as well as the master and the owner of the ship, that serious danger lay ahead. But disregarding the advice of a prisoner, the centurion listened to the master and the owner of the ship and set sail from Crete notwithstanding.

The account of the terrific struggle with the raging sea is one of the most exciting in ancient literature. A short time after the harbor of Fair Havens in Crete was quitted a tempestuous wind, called Euraquilo, beat down upon the ship and for fourteen days and nights spun it like a top on a wild sea, threatening momentarily to break it in pieces and plunge its occupants into a watery grave.

As the crew "labored exceedingly with the storm" (Acts 27:18) and realized in their utterly futile efforts that imminent death faced them, the conviction of the worthlessness of things was borne in upon their consciousness. Accordingly, "they began to throw the freight overboard" on the second day, "and the third day they cast out with their own hands the tackling of the ship" (Acts 27:18, 19).

For the two hundred and seventy-six souls aboard the tempest-tossed vessel the eleven days that followed constituted an ineradicable experience of hopeless despair and starless night. "And when neither sun nor stars shone upon us for many days," wrote the inspired historian, "and no small tempest lay on us, all hope that we should be saved was now taken away" (Acts 27:20).

STARS FOR THE STORMY NIGHT

There was one man aboard ship, however, to whom this terrible night-time experience was neither starless nor hopeless. And so protracted and fearful was the tempest, that even he would have despaired of life had not God graciously hung out special lamps of hope to illuminate the darkness and encourage His faithful servant.

This gruelling time of suffering and testing for the Apostle Paul revealed his moral greatness and brought with it the vision of God to cheer him, that he might in turn cheer others. As Paul stood forth in the midst of the storm-battered exhausted voyagers, his words had the ring and the assurance of one who, in the agony of suffering, had "seen God face to face," like Jacob at Peniel, and like the patriarch of old, his life had "been preserved" (Gen. 32:30).

"And now I exhort you to be of good cheer; for there shall be no loss of life among you, but only of the ship. For there stood by me this night an angel of the Lord whose I am, whom also I serve, saying, Fear not, Paul; thou must stand before Caesar: and lo, God hath granted thee all them that sail with thee. Wherefore, sirs, be of good cheer: for I

believe God, that it shall be even so as it hath been
spoken unto me" (Acts 27:22-25).

The Apostle was not only immeasurably blessed
himself by the experience of the storm, but he
was enabled to be an incalculable blessing to the two
hundred seventy-six souls on board the ship with him.
To be able to stand before them in their sheer ex-
haustion and utter hopelessness and assure them "to
be of good cheer" was in itself a triumph of God's
goodness. To have his words accompanied by calm
certainty and the assurance of heaven was to their
fear-ridden hearts like a comforting voice from another world singing "Songs in the Night."

> *Sweeter words, I think, were never spoken,*
> *Nor words that shine with more unfailing light,*
> *A healing balm to lend when hearts are broken,*
> *Brave words—"He giveth songs in the night."*
>
> *His presence makes the shadows bright with singing*
> *And every fear takes wing in certain flight,*
> *Oh, keep the words of hope forever ringing:*
> *"God giveth songs—He giveth songs in the night."*
>
> *Friend of the midnight road that knows no turning,*
> *God's promises are sure; His will is right,*
> *Beyond the storm a million stars are burning;*
> *And he will keep you singing in the night!*
> —S. L. Armes

In that dark hour God's faithful witness, account-
ed worthy to suffer for the name of Jesus Christ, was
in a most beautiful manner demonstrating God's purpose in the trials of His people, namely; that they may
not only see the stars of God's love and grace them-

selves when the dark starless night of affliction is upon them, but also that they may be able to sing songs in the night and to point others to the lamps of divine goodness hung aloft to relieve the gloom of adversity and testing.

Out of a wealth of such varicolored experiences of suffering and hardship the Apostle was himself prepared to write to the afflicted saints at Corinth on the divine purpose of such trials. His important instruction to them takes the form of a benediction. "Blessed be the God and Father of our Lord Jesus Christ, the Father of mercies and God of all comfort; who comforteth us in all our affliction, that we may be able to comfort them that are in any affliction, through the comfort wherewith we ourselves are comforted of God" (2 Cor. 1:3, 4).

The multiplied dangers and trials through which Paul had passed in his long and faithful ministry for Christ were now bearing fruit in his calm deportment and remarkable ministry of comfort in the vortex of the raging tempest.

When the sailors at midnight on the fourteenth day of the storm realized that the ship was being rapidly driven toward land, and there was great consternation as soundings were made, the Apostle with admirable self-control advised that unless those who were attempting to leave the ship by a life-boat remained on board, they could not be saved. His calm self-assurance so impressed the centurion and the soldiers that they "cut away the ropes of the boat, and let her fall off" (Acts 27:32).

STARLIGHT AND BREAKING DAY

"And while the day was coming on, Paul besought them all to take some food, saying, This day is the fourteenth day that ye wait and continue fasting, having taken nothing. Wherefore I beseech you to take some food: for this is for your safety: for there shall not a hair perish from the head of any of you" (Acts 27:33, 34).

The moral courage of the Apostle, even though he was a prisoner, automatically made him an undisputed leader in the crisis that was at hand. The deep inner tranquility of heart, the result of the vision of God to his soul, imparted to him a fearlessness of behavior which the desperate fear-ridden crew ready to grasp at any straw of hope, found exceedingly attractive.

Having assured the passengers and crew that all would be well, and having urged them to take food in token of their impending deliverance, a dramatic moment follows when Paul, as the starless darkness of night receded, took bread and "gave thanks to God in the presence of all, and . . . break it, and began to eat" (Acts 27:35).

The spirit of contagious hopefulness and assured optimism that characterized him spread to all on the storm-battered boat as the dawning light of the new day that was breaking gave fresh courage. "Then were they all of good cheer and themselves also took food" (Acts 27:36). The entire two hundred and seventy-six people on the vessel had their morale wonderfully lifted and faith and hope engendered in their hearts by one man who knew and served the living God. He could hang out stars in the starless stormy night and point the way to breaking day because he knew the Maker of the stars and, like Jacob, when his name was changed to Israel, "had power with God and with men" (Gen. 32:28 marg.).

With their minds and hearts strengthened by faith and hope and their physical bodies reinvigorated by food, the passengers and crew of the ill-fated vessel were able to gird themselves for the final ordeal eventuating in deliverance from the fury of the sea. With the forepart of the ship wedged in the rocks, and the hinder part being broken to pieces by the violence of the waves, all the people, whether by swimming to shore or floating on planks and debris from the wrecked ship, escaped safely to land.

One man of God, found faithful to the will of God, could not only sight stars in a starless night of storm, but point others to these lamps of God's grace and be an instrument of blessing and deliverance to all who were with him in the perilous experience. Fourteen terrible sunless days and fourteen dreadful starless nights of pitiless pelting by a wildly raging sea brought rich benefit to God's servant and to those to whom he ministered.

When the darkness had given way to light, when the lashing of the wind-swept tumultuous waves was only a past memory as the safety of the land was reached, the Apostle, and doubtless many of those to whom he ministered during the ordeal of the storm could say, "O, blessed storm, thou hast brought me to the knowledge of Christ! O happy starless night, thou hast conducted me to the light of life! O tumultuous sea, thou hast tossed me furiously on thy bosom only to bring me to rest on the bosom of God!"

> *Like the sweet dawn of the morning,*
> *Like the sweet freshness of dew,*
> *Comes the dear whisper of Jesus,*
> *Comforting, tender and true.*
> *Darkness gives way to the sunlight,*
> *While His voice falls on my ear;*
> *Seasons of heaven's refreshing*
> *Call to new gladness and cheer.*

> *Whispering hope,*
> *Like the song of the angels,*
> *Jesus, Thy love*
> *Is sweet music to me.*

DIVINE JUDGMENTS AND FALLING STARS

> *But immediately after the tribulation of those days the sun shall be darkened, and the moon shall not give her light, and the stars shall fall from heaven, and the powers of the heavens shall be shaken* (Matt. 24:29)

In Scripture divine judgment upon sin is frequently connected with far-reaching celestial upheavals, such as falling stars, darkened sun and moon and other portents. The fiery prophet Amos denounced the idolatry and vari-colored iniquities of Israel in his day and foretold sidereal commotions. "Shall not the land tremble for this," he cried, "and everyone mourn that dwelleth therein? . . . And it shall come to pass in that day, saith the Lord Jehovah, that I will cause the sun to go down at noon, and I will darken the earth in a clear day" (Amos 8:8, 9).

Ezekiel in pronouncing judgment upon the pharaoh of Egypt graphically prophecies the doom of that proud and wicked monarch in terms of heavenly commotions. "And when I shall extinguish thee, I will cover the heavens, and make the stars thereof dark; I will cover the sun with a cloud, and the moon shall not give its light. All the bright lights of heaven will I make dark over thee, and set darkness upon thy land, saith the Lord Jehovah" (Ezek. 32:7, 8).

Signs in the Stars

The prophetic Word reveals that the ending of this present age preceding the second advent of Christ and the establishment of the millennial kingdom will be a period of world-wide trouble heralded by cosmic disturbances. Just as the first coming of our Lord in mercy and salvation was attended by signs in the heavens and the guiding star conducting The Wise-Men to the Babe of Bethlehem, so the second coming of the Lord in wrath and judgment upon His enemies will be accompanied by terrific shaking of the powers of the heavens.

Matthew's gospel reveals that "immediately after the tribulation of those days the sun shall be darkened, and the moon shall not give her light, and the stars shall fall from heaven, and the powers of the heavens shall be shaken" (Matt. 24:29). This terrific quaking in the heavenly realms is most intimately connected with the glorious appearance of Christ. "And then shall appear the sign of the Son of Man in heaven: and then shall all the tribes of the earth mourn, and they shall see the Son of man coming on the clouds of heaven with power and great glory" (Matt. 24:30).

Our Lord's Olivet Discourse not only relates the tribulation period to the ending of the age and His second advent, but stresses its unprecedented severity and world-wide extent. "For then shall be great tribulation, such as hath not been from the beginning of the world until now, no, nor ever shall be" (Matt. 24:21).

Our Lord's important prophecy enunciating the fact of the tribulation does not stand alone. It is amply attested by numerous other prophecies both in the Old and New Testament. Various references to this end-time upheaval show that it is a period of judgment primarily affecting the Jews, refining them preparatory to their reinstatement into divine favor in the coming age.

Jeremiah notably describes the tribulation as the time of "Jacob's trouble" (Jer. 30:7). So intense is it that "every man" is pictured "with his hands on his loins, as a woman in travail, and all faces are turned into paleness" (Jer. 30:6). Like Jesus, Jeremiah stresses its unprecedented greatness. "Alas! for that day is great, so that none is like it. . . ." (Jer. 30:7).

Daniel also envisioned the period as "a time of trouble, such as never was since there was a nation even to that same time" and relates it to his own people, the Jews, who "at that time . . . shall be delivered, everyone that shall be found written in the book" (Dan. 12:1).

Ezekiel also pictures the dreadful time of judgment as the period when Israel shall "pass under the rod" and God "will purge out" from among them "the rebels and them that transgress" (Ezek. 20:37, 38). He also delineates it as a fiery refining process when God "will blow" upon them with "the fire" of His wrath (Ezek. 22:21). Zechariah describes the same process when Israel shall be cast into God's refining crucible and be purified as silver and tried "as gold is tried" (Zech. 13:9).

Although the great tribulation will be primarily a refining process upon the Jew preparing him for reinstatement into divine favor and millennial blessing, it will affect the Gentile nations of the world as well. But the church of Christ will not be concerned with these dreadful apocalyptic judgments having been glorified and translated to heaven before the outbreak of this stormy trial (1 Thess. 4:13-18; 2 Thess. 2:1-4).

The New Testament presents two extended passages on this period of storm and world-wide trouble. The first is by Jesus in His great Olivet Discourse (Matt. 24:9-22) and the second by John, comprising the bulk of the book of the Revelation (6:1-19:21).

In the Olivet Discourse our Lord emphasizes the sidereal commotions accompanying these catastrophic earth-judgments. In the parallel account in Mark the same emphasis prevails. "But in those days, after that tribulation, the sun shall be darkened, and the moon shall not give her light, and the stars shall be falling from heaven, and the powers that are in the heavens shall be shaken. And then shall they see the Son of man coming in clouds with great power and glory" (Mark 13:24-26).

In the Lukan account our Lord, having foretold the fall of Jerusalem in 70 A.D. (Luke 21:20-24), bridges the gap of this present period of Jewish unbelief and dispersion, and returns to the end of the age when "the times of the Gentiles" have been fulfilled (Luke 21:24) and God again takes up with Israel.

In reference to the events of the tribulation our Lord, as in the accounts in Matthew and Mark, speaks of celestial signs. "And there shall be signs in the sun and moon and stars" (Luke 21:25). These omens in the heavens are accompanied by vast physical and social upheavals on the earth. "And upon the earth distress of nations, in perplexity for the roaring of the sea and the billows; men fainting for fear, and for expectation of the things which are coming on the world: for the powers of the heavens shall be shaken" (Luke 21:25, 26).

Signs in the sun and moon and stars! Perplexity among nations! Men fainting for fear! The powers of the heavens shaken! Awful judgments poured out upon Christ-rejecting earth dwellers! This is the fearful scene that marks man's iniquity when it has reached its peak and is ripe for the full manifestation of the divine wrath and the loosing of the terrible storm of God's unmitigated fury.

FALLING STARS AND OUTPOURED WRATH

The most extended and detailed account of what is to occur in the end-time period of world-wide trouble is found in the book of the Revelation (6:1-19:21). The "seven-sealed book," which the Lamb

opens (Rev. 5:1-7) is the title-deed and legal right
to the redeemed earth secured by Christ as a result
of His death on the cross. John the Revelator sees
the Redeemer open the document and take possession
of the earth according to its provisions. The breaking
of the seven seals (which include the trumpet and the
vial judgments) eventuates in the complete purging
out of Satan and sinners from the earth, climaxed by
the glorious advent of Christ and the establishment
of the millennial kingdom.

Each of the seven seals, trumpets and vials com-
prises a terrible divine judgment let loose upon a
Satan-dominated earth and upon wicked Christ-rejecting earth-dwellers. Many of these apocalyptic judgments fall upon the heavens as well, until both the
celestial spheres (now defiled by the presence of Satan
and his evil angels) and the earth, are fully purged for
the inauguration of the coming age. Satan and evil
angels are expelled from the heavenlies and remanded
to the abyss (Rev. 20:1-5), while Christ-rejecting Jews
and Gentiles are destroyed.

The whole series of dreadful apocalyptic judgments
are like a violent storm that bursts in fury at dusk and
rages with increased violence all night long. Torrential rains inundate the land, furious winds fell stout
trees, livid lightning splinters the mighty oaks and
thunder crashes against the mountainside.

But when morning dawns the world is rain-washed
and clean. Yonder birch shimmers in rustling beauty
in the breeze. Each flower and blade of grass in the
meadow is bathed and scented like a fairy princess

fresh from her boudoir. The brook runs clear and bright with every stagnant waterhole cleansed, and the river passing the great metropolis is purified as its foul contagion is swept out to sea, lost in the limitless expanse of the ocean.

Amidst the various seals involving such calamities as war, famine and death is the sixth seal. The loosing of this mighty judgment produces a globe-extending earthquake in which "every mountain and island" is "moved out of its places" (Rev. 6:14). Concomitant with this earthly cataclysm is a gigantic shaking of the heavens. The sun becomes "black as sackcloth of hair," the moon "as blood" and the stars of the heaven "fall" unto the earth, as a fig tree casteth her unripe fruit when she is shaken of a great wind." And the heaven is "removed as a scroll when it is rolled up" (Rev. 6:12-14).

Darkened sun and moon and falling stars are the same portents of divine judgment alluded to by our Lord in the Olivet Discourse (Matt. 24:29). So terrifying is the shaking of the heavens and the earth in this divine visitation that wicked earth-dwellers hide themselves "in the caves and rocks of the mountains: and they say to the mountains and to the rocks, Fall on us, and hide us from the face of him that sitteth on the throne, and from the wrath of the Lamb; for the great day of their wrath is come; and who is able to stand?" (Rev. 6:15-17).

The potential destructiveness of modern nuclear weapons of warfare devised by man is striking terror to millions of people the world over. But what must be the paralyzing fear struck in the hearts of Christ-hating humanity when the God of all power, the Creator of the atom and He who holds the universe together in the palm of His hand arises to manifest His full wrath against Christ-rejecting men. Sinners will not be able to stand before the blaze of the divine anger as the sidereal heavens are violently shaken and an earthquake-ridden globe is showered with fiery meteors. The unrepentant and fearful will cry deliriously for the rocks and mountains to cover them and protect them from the wrath of the Lamb in the day when the storm of His fury breaks.

A Blazing Star and Bitter Waters

The fearful trumpet judgments of the book of the Revelation follow the seals. The third and fourth trumpets involve the heavenly bodies. "And the third angel sounded, and there fell from heaven *a great star,* burning as a torch, and it fell upon the third part of the rivers, and upon the fountains of the waters; and *the name of the star is called Wormwood*: and the third part of the waters became wormwood; and many men died of the waters, because they were made bitter" (Rev. 8:10, 11).

The description of this *"great star blazing as a torch"* apparently identifies it with a huge meteor. Striking the air of our planet this great body will explode, enveloping earth's atmosphere with deadly gases. These poisonous vapors will be absorbed by the rivers and sources of water, making them extremely bitter and causing widespread death to those who drink them.

The star is named Wormwood because the effect

it has upon the sources of water is like the wormwood plant, especially that variety celebrated for its intensely bitter quality, used to flavor an aromatic liqueur called absinthe, popular in France. Several varieties of wormwood are found in Syria-Palestine, and it is easy for men to see in this cataclysmic judgment the fact that they are reaping the bitter fruits of sin in this heaven-sent visitation.

Smitten Stars and Upset Science

The fourth trumpet following upon the third announces another judgment involving the heavenly bodies. "And the fourth angel sounded, and the third part of the sun was smitten, and the third part of the moon, and the *third part of the stars;* that the third part of them should be darkened, and the day should not shine for the third part of it, and the night in like manner" (Rev. 8:12).

When our Lord plainly foretold that "the powers of the heavens shall be shaken" (Luke 21:26), He evidently had reference to the temporary setting aside of the normal physical laws of the universe, such as gravitation and planetary attraction. These scientifically unexplainable "signs" or supernatural portents "in the sun and moon and stars" announcing the second advent of Christ as the cataclysmic event of the ages, will cause universal consternation among men who do not know and who do not desire to know God.

There is a piercing blast of a trumpet, and lo! out goes the sun! Daylight, contrary to all the physical laws of this universe, turns into night! *And such night!* Impenetrable darkness—starless, moonless, fearfully black. Then lo! again the sun shines! And unbelieving men, whose confidence is in their own knowledge and in "science," are transfixed with terror.

Human reliance in "the unchangeableness of material law" and in "all things" continuing "as they were from the beginning of the creation" (2 Pet. 3:4) is rudely shattered. Mockers of the idea of the second coming of Christ are suddenly jolted out of their naturalistic and materialistic groove. The "distress of nations, in perplexity for the roaring of the sea and the billows" is the terrifying horror gripping men because no science will be able to explain these apocalyptic phenomena.

Men will be "fainting for fear, and for expectation of the things which are coming upon the earth" as they see "the powers of the heavens . . . shaken" (Luke 21:26). At last the shrine of naturalistic science at which human intellect has so long bowed and worshipped the god of natural forces, and from whose sanctum the supernatural and the miraculous have been barred as profane, shall now lie in ruins at the feet of unbelieving men. And having ruled God out of their lives, they will have no place of refuge to which to turn, but only to blind despair and paralyzing fear.

STAR-ANGEL CUSTODIAN AND DISPRISONED DEMONS

The fifth trumpet of the Revelation, like the third and fourth, mentions a heavenly luminary. In this case, however, the "star" alluded to is not a literal star, but an angel who is the keeper of "the pit of the abyss," the prison house of the demons. John saw this *"star from heaven fallen unto the earth"* "and given

the key of the pit of the abyss," with which he un-
locked the place of confinement of myriads of evil
spirits. The star-angel is evidently the same angelic
personage who binds Satan (and the demons) in the
abyss during the kingdom age (Rev. 20:1-3).

As the angel-custodian unlocks the abyss, millions
of demon-spirits in the form of scorpion-locusts are un-
loosed to afflict and torment wicked earthdwellers during the tribulation and to goad them on in their opposition to God and His Christ (Rev. 9:1-11).

The Apostle John glimpsed the denizens of the evil
spirit-world by supernatural vision. The hideous com-
posite scorpion-locusts which he saw, however, as well
as the frog-like evil spirits sent forth later to drive
ungodly men on to Armageddon (Rev. 16:13-16) will
be invisible to the natural eye. Their presence will be
known by the intense suffering they inflict, the powerful dynamic for evil-doing they impart, and the gross
deception they cause.

The present age of the church is a period of widespread demon activity (1 Tim. 4:1; 1 John 4:1, 2),
but it is to a large extent curbed by the restraining
ministry of the Holy Spirit resident in and operating
through the church, the body of Christ, and by the
fact that many of the most vicious and wicked demons
are now imprisoned.

The action of the star-angel of Revelation in un-
locking the abyss, represents the freeing of millions of
these unclean God-hating spirits to indwell men and
drive them on in their God-defying blasphemies at the
ending of the age. It is a divine punishment upon

men who have refused the light. "And for this cause God sendeth them a working of error, that they should believe a lie; that they all might be judged who believed not the truth, but had pleasure in unrighteousness" (2 Thess. 2:11, 12).

STAR-CROWNED WOMAN AND MAN-CHILD

In the twelfth chapter of the Revelation the Apostle John saw "a great sign" or symbol "in heaven: a woman arrayed with the sun, and the moon under her feet *and upon her head a crown of twelve stars*" (Rev. 12:1). This star-crowned woman symbolizes the nation Israel. The imagery harks back to Joseph's celebrated dream (Gen. 37:9) in which he saw his father and mother (the sun and the moon) and his eleven brothers (the eleven stars) bowing down to him (the twelfth star).

Hence it is plain that the crown of *twelve stars* upon the head of the sun-arrayed woman of Revelation 12 speaks of millennially restored Israel in full governmental blessing, manifesting the rule of the heavens upon the earth, and bringing fulfilment of the petition "Thy kingdom come. Thy will be done in earth, as it is in heaven" (Matt. 6:10).

The fact that the woman is sun-clothed indicates that she is enveloped with Christ the light of the world (John 8:12) as the result of her acceptance of Him at His second advent and her full spiritual restoration.

But the symbol is panoramic as the other "signs" of this chapter and spans the centuries. The woman is seen "with child, and she crieth out, travailing in birth to be delivered . . . and she was delivered of a

Son, a man child, who is to rule all the nations with a rod of iron: and her child was caught up unto God, and unto his throne" (Rev. 12:2, 5).

The man-child is Christ Who was born of Israel, of which nation Paul said: "Of whom is Christ as concerning the flesh" (Rom. 9:5). Israel's constant expectation was for the time when she could say, "Unto us a child is born, unto us a son is given" (Isa. 9:7).

The second Psalm clearly indicates that the man-child brought forth in Israel's travail, is Christ:

> *I will tell of the decree:*
> *Jehovah said unto me, Thou art my son;*
> *This day have I begotten thee.*
> *Ask of me, and I will give thee the nations for thine*
>   *inheritance,*
> *And the uttermost parts of the earth for thy possession.*
> *Thou shalt break them with a rod of iron;*
> *Thou shalt dash them in pieces like a potter's vessel*
>   (Psa. 2:7-9).

The symbol of the woman, Israel, giving birth to the man-child harks back in the history of the nation to the birth of Christ in order to connect Him with the Jewish people in the darkest hour of the fierce tribulation tempest about to burst upon them in unmitigated fury, as the context of chapter 12 demonstrates. This close association of the Messiah with His elect people Israel reveals the deep interest He takes in them always, but especially in their time of supreme suffering.

THE DRAGON AND THE STARS OF HEAVEN

"And there was another sign in heaven: and behold, a great red dragon, having seven heads and ten horns, and upon his heads seven diadems. *And his tail draweth the third part of the stars of heaven, and did cast them to the earth"* (Rev. 12:3, 4).

The dragon is "the old serpent the Devil and Satan, the deceiver of the whole world" (Rev. 12:9). His color is red, the color of blood, for "he was a murderer from the beginning" (John 8:44). *"The stars of heaven"* attached to the Dragon's tail are the angels Satan led in revolt in the pristine rebellion, in the Old Testament angels being called "stars" (Job 38:7). Satan himself in his unfallen splendor was styled "the day-star, son of the morning" (Isa. 14:12).

The symbol of the dragon, like that of the woman, is panoramic in scope. It traces Satan's career from his primeval fall in the dim past to the final earth-rule through ten confederated kings, directed by seven heads. He is seen standing before the woman Israel to devour her child Christ, as soon as He was born. He is also visualized cast out of heaven and upon the earth (Rev. 12:7-17).

Cast upon the earth with his evil angels, who are expelled from the heavenlies with him, and aided by augmented demon forces let loose from the abyss (Rev. 9:1-21), Satan stages his last and most terrible attack against Israel. His purpose is to annihilate God's covenant people and frustrate Christ's plan to rule over the earth through them.

In this violent and relentlessly cruel campaign against Israel and against any who may in that day name the name of Christ, Satan displays in himself all the horror and stark barbarity contained in the figure of "the dragon," with its tail drawing "the third part of the stars of heaven" to assist him in his nefarious plan. His supreme attempt to take over the earth for himself, however, ends in abysmal failure, as he is cast into the abyss at the glorious advent of the all-conquering Christ, coming upon the clouds of heaven in terrible splendor as "King of kings and Lord of lords" to exterminate the last rebellious foe and rule in righteousness and peace without a rival.

> *Wonderful hope, He is coming again,*
> *Coming as King o'er the nations to reign;*
> *Glorious promise, His Word cannot fail,*
> *His righteous kingdom at last must prevail!*
>
> *Wonderful name He bears,*
> *Wonderful crown He wears,*
> *Wonderful blessings His triumphs afford;*
> *Wonderful Calvary,*
> *Wonderful grace for me,*
> *Wonderful love of my Wonderful Lord!*
> A. H. Ackley

STARLIT PATH TO THE SAVIOR

Chapter Six

The Bright, The Morning Star

I am the root and the offspring of David, the bright, the morning star (Rev. 22:16).

THE STAR OUT OF JACOB

. . . There shall come forth a star out of Jacob,
And a sceptre shall rise out of Israel . . . (Num. 24:17).

The witness of the Holy Spirit as the "spirit of prophecy," which is "the testimony of Jesus" (Rev. 19:10), to the coming of the Savior, is like the appearance of stars of the night, and finally the breaking of dawn and the rising of the sun dispelling the darkness and ushering in the full light of a new day. The entrance of sin into the human family plunged man into midnight darkness and exposed him to sorrow, pain, physical as well as spiritual death and all the tragic consequences of alienation from God.

Immediately after man's fall, however, the grace of God began to move in tender compassion and love to restore him to divine fellowship and relieve the pall of spiritual night that had settled down upon the human soul. The Spirit of God, who had "moved upon the face of the waters" in the chaotic globe and brought order out of confusion, now as the Spirit of prophecy began to stir in bringing "the testimony of Jesus" as Messiah and Savior to lost man.

The first bright star of light piercing the deep gloom of man's spiritual night was God's announcement of glorious hope contained in the so-called *Protevangelium* or "first gospel." It was uttered in connection with the serpent-tempter's doom and foretells the gigantic struggle between Christ, the woman's "seed" or descendant, and Antichrist, the serpent's "seed" with the final complete triumph of the former (Gen. 3:15).

The Holy Spirit progressively revealed other Messianic promises and hopes centering in the coming Redeemer. Each succeeding prediction added details and traced out the expanding pattern of God's redemptive plan till not only was man's sin-darkened sky filled with luminous promises, but ascending rays of light appeared presaging the dawn and the rising "Sun of righteousness" heralding the full brightness of the millennial day (Mal. 4:2).

BALAAM'S STAR-PROPHECY

One of the most beautifully suggestive prophetic foregleams of Messiah in the entire Bible was uttered by the semi-heathen diviner Balaam. Coming under the mighty sway of the Spirit of God, he was constrained, despite his pagan background and the godless pressures brought to bear upon him contrariwise, to announce some of the most glowing predictions of Israel's coming Deliverer and future blessing to be found anywhere in Scripture.

> *I see him. but not now;*
> *I behold him, but not nigh.*
> *There shall come forth a star out of Jacob,*
> *And a sceptre shall rise out of Israel,*
> *And shall smite through the corners of Moab,*
> *And break down all the sons of tumult* (Num. 24:17).

The vision of the diviner-prophet spans the limitless centuries and glimpses a far-distant vista. Darkness appears. The nocturnal skies are black, without a single luminary. Then of a sudden a star arises—an extraordinary star—large, exquisitely clear and dazzlingly brilliant. It fills the horizon. It captivates the prophet's vision. It represents unmistakably the rise of a glorious ruler or king to ascend "out of Jacob" in the nightime of his descendants' experience when their skies are black and starless.

Entranced by the fine lustre and radiant splendor of the star, and filled with awe and reverence at the royal personage it symbolized, the excited seer cries out:

> *I see Him, but not now;*
> *I behold Him, but not nigh.*

Balaam was thus vouchsafed in this his fourth and final prophecy a far-distant revelation of Israel's future. It was specifically a disclosure of what they would do "in the latter days" when their Messiah would come and establish His millennial kingdom over them and conquer all their enemies (Num. 24:14). This long-range view is corroborated not only by the prophet's own words, but by his use of this distinctive millennial title of our Lord . . . "the Most High":

> *He saith, Who heareth the words of God,*
> *And knoweth the knowledge of the Most High?*

Although in this particular prophetic foregleam the sombre darkness of Israel's unbelief and rejection furnishes the background against which the "star out of Jacob" arises, the night is evidently waning and dawn is near, for one of the very brightest of the morning stars is apparently intended. These, the latest stars to appear in the Eastern sky before sunrise, were the heralds of the dawn. The prophet apparently envisioned one of these exceedingly luminous bodies which was last to rise before its shining was drowned in the glowing light of day.

Could there be any more picturesque representation of the Messiah than as a splendid luminous morning-star announcing His sunrise appearance to His people; effecting their conversion and their entrance into full millennial blessing? The whole prophetic preview, moreover, looks to the time when the "Jacob" character of God's ancient covenant people is about to give way to their "Israel" character. Only as they see and own their Redeemer at His second advent will their unbelieving and "supplanting" spirit give way to "a prince-with-God" spirit, as in the case of their patriarchal progenitor when he saw "God face to face" at Peniel (Gen. 32:30).

A star is a natural symbol of imperial greatness and splendor and was commonly employed in this sense in the ancient Near East. The belief also was widely held that the birth and accession of great kings was made known by the appearance of stars.

Not only stars, but the celestial bodies in general —sun, moon and planets, as well as light, splendor and day were considered as emblems of royalty and imperial government. Numerous royal personages both men and women, therefore, had these names given to them as titles and surnames.

Hadassah, who became Ahasuerus' queen, was called Sitareh or Esther, meaning "star," and from which our common English word was developed by corruption. Alexander the Great's queen, called Roxana by the Greeks was named *Roushen,* "splendor" in her native Persian tongue. A certain Mohammedan prince named Joseph, upon elevation to the throne, was styled *Roushen Akhter,* which signifies a "splendid" or "luminous star."

THE SCEPTRE OF THE STAR-KING

Any doubt that the ascending star represents the appearance of a glorious ruler or king is removed by the parallel declaration "and a sceptre shall rise out of Israel" (Num. 24:17). The star-king is the sceptre-bearer. He comes forth out of Jacob and Israel as a star to denote his glory and splendor and as a sceptre-bearer to signify his power and authority. It is He who shall have dominion.

The figure of the Messianic sceptre had already figured prominently in Jacob's earlier prophecy concerning his sons:

> *The sceptre shall not depart from Judah*
> *Nor the ruler's staff from between his feet,*
> *Until Shiloh come,*
> *And unto him shall the obedience of the peoples be*
>   **(Gen. 49:10).**

Dying Jacob glimpsed by prophetic vision that the sceptre should come into the tribe of Judah (fulfilled in David) and that Shiloh, David's seed, and the Promised Seed, the Savior, should also come out of that tribe in which governmental authority should continue until after Messiah's first advent.

Balaam, however, in his prophecy of the sceptre-bearing star-king, unlike Jacob, sees Messiah *not* in His first advent in humiliation and rejection, but in His glorious second coming in judgment to smite His enemies, rule the nations "with a rod of iron" and reign as "King of kings and Lord of lords" (Rev. 19:15, 16).

The sceptre that is prophecied to arise out of Israel is said to

> . . . *Smite through the corners of Moab,*
> *And break down all the sons of tumult,*
> *And Edom shall be a possession,*
> *Seir also shall be a possession, who were his enemies;*
> *While Israel doeth valiantly* (Num. 24:17, 18).

In David's time this prophecy was partially or typically realized. Israel's great conqueror and type of Messiah "smote Moab, and measured them with the line, making them to lie down on the ground; and he measured two lines to put to death, and one full line to keep alive" (2 Sam. 8:2). David's severe treatment of the Moabites prefigured the Messianic rule "with a rod of iron" when He dashes His enemy "in pieces like a potter's vessel" (Psa. 2:9), and treads "the wine press of the fury of the wrath of God the Almighty" (Rev. 19:15).

A later inspired psalmist had a marvelous revelation of the reign of the sceptre-bearing star-king envisioned by Balaam. He delineates Messianic administration as a rule of benign peace and blessing upon the righteous, but a regime of terrible severity as far as the unrighteous are concerned:

> *He will come down like rain upon the mown grass,*
> *As showers that water the earth.*
> *In his days shall the righteous flourish,*
> *And abundance of peace, till the moon be no more.*
> *He shall have dominion also from sea to sea*
> *And from the River unto the ends of the earth.*
> *They that dwell in the wilderness shall bow before him;*
> *And his enemies shall lick the dust.*
> *The kings of Tarshish and the isles shall render tribute:*
> *The kings of Sheba and Seba shall offer gifts.*
> *Yea, all kings shall fall down before him;*
> *All nations shall serve him* (Psa. 72:6-11).

David's extensive but limited conquests prefigured Messiah's millennial reign. Messiah's sceptre-sway, however, will be world-wide. *"All* kings shall fall down before him, *all* nations shall serve him" (Psa. 72:11). Balaam saw the star-king's conquests principally in terms of Israel's enemies at the time, but the sweep of His inspired vision spanned the centuries and glimpsed Messiah's final conquest over *all* Israel's enemies.

THE STAR-KING AND THE NEST AMONG THE STARS

Balaam not only predicted that the sceptre of the star-king would smite through Moab, but also that another of Israel's inveterate enemies, Edom, should become "a possession" of victorious Israel.

> *And Edom shall be a possession,*
> *Seir also shall be a possession,*
>   *Who were his enemies;*
> *While Israel doeth valiantly*
> *And out of Jacob shall one have dominion,*
> *And shall destroy the remnant of the city*
>   (Num. 24:18, 19).

This prophecy, like that concerning Moab, received a typical fulfilment in David who subdued Edom and garrisoned the country. "And all the Edomites became servants to David" (2 Sam. 8:14). But the ultimate accomplishment of this prediction is to be found in the conquests of Messiah, star-king, at His second advent in glory.

The prophet Obadiah had a similar but far-more detailed vision of Edom's destruction in the latter days and Israel's exaltation in Messiah's coming kingdom. Graphically Obadiah refers to Edom's implacable hatred of God's people Israel, her impregnable position in the rocky sandstone cliffs and fastness of Petra, and her eventual doom.

"The pride of thy heart hath deceived thee, O thou that dwellest in the clefts of the rock, whose habitation is high; that saith in thy heart, Who shall bring me down to the ground?" (Obad. 1:3).

But the answer of God's wrath against the representative enemy of his people is: "Though thou mount on high as the eagle, and *though thy nest be set among the stars,* I will bring thee down from thence, saith Jehovah" (Obad. 1:4).

Nestled among their lofty crags and gorgeously colored precipices, and securely intrenched in their virtually impregnable rock-cut rose-hued citadel, the Edomites superciliously disdained God's people, Israel, and boasted in their physical safety. They proudly called their fortress-city "the Rock," rendered "Petra" by the Greeks and "Selah" (Isa. 16:1) by the Hebrews.

To the Old Testament seer the Edomites represented the acme of pride and carnal self-security and epitomized the bitterest hatred against the people of God. As the prophet's prophetic vision sweeps over the centuries and envisions the coming of Israel's Messianic deliverer, he sees complete defeat for all such foes of God and God's program.

Though they, like Edom, build themselves a stronghold in the highest crags, and like the eagle build their "nest" in the loftiest and most inaccessible fissures of the rocks, yet God will find out their place of security and destroy them. Though they might even set their nest "among the stars" thousands of light years away, "I will bring thee down from thence, saith Jehovah" (Obad. 1:4).

In the coming "day of Jehovah" (Obad. 1:15) when the Lord will "restore the kingdom to Israel" (Acts 1:6), the sceptre-wielding star-king of Balaam's prophecy, the mighty all-conquering Christ, will "exalt that which is low, and abase that which is high" (Ezek. 21:26). "For, behold, the day cometh, it shall burn as a furnace; and all the proud and all that work wickedness shall be as stubble; and the day that cometh shall burn them up, saith Jehovah of hosts, that it shall leave them neither root nor branch" (Mal. 4:1).

THE STAR IN THE EAST

The birth of Christ was heralded in a supernatural manner not only to Jews by the visitation of angelic messengers to humble Bethlehem shepherds but also to Gentiles by the appearance of a star. This star was directly connected with the birth of Messiah because it

was said by the visiting Magi to be "his star" (Matt.
2:1) and therefore must have been supernatural. Attempts have been made to describe "the star" as a
conjunction of planets, a comet, a variable star, or a
meteor.

The narrative apparently purposely leaves the star-
phenomenon astronomically incomplete, either to im-
ply its totally supernatural character or to suggest
that the star, no matter what its physical nature, was
of no consequence except as a guide to the birthplace
of the infant Jesus.

The question has often been asked whether
Balaam's prophecy "there shall come forth a star out
of Jacob" and "a sceptre shall rise out of Israel" (Num.
24:17) is to be connected with Messiah's star which
the Magi saw and which announced Christ's birth.
The answer would seem to be that it seems perfectly
reasonable to suppose that this great Messianic prophecy had been preserved in Mesopotamia, whence
Balaam came, and may with further divine revelations,
have furnished the core of truth upon which the Magi
acted.

It is certainly a pleasing thought that these devout
Gentiles had treasured and meditated upon a prophecy
given by one who may well have been a member of a
priestly order allied to themselves. These noble "wise
men from the East" assuredly had lived up to the
light they had, and found themselves recipients of more
light, even the brilliant lustre of a luminous star shining through the darkness and leading them to worship
Him Who was "born King of the Jews" (Matt. 2:3).

The Magi of Matthew's gospel were among those whom God has "in every nation" that fear him and work righteousness and who are "acceptable to him" (Acts 10:35). As followers of Zoroaster, they rejected polytheism and idolatry, and in principle were worshippers of the one only God. Their simple creed and singularly high code of morality, which Zoroastrianism in its purest form professed, were eminently conducive to prepare its faithful followers to receive an added revelation, as in the case of the Magi, who were directed by a wondrous star to the Savior-King at Bethlehem.

These so-called "wise men" were wise men indeed. In the first place, they sought the Savior; in the second place, they sought Him until they found Him; in the third place, when they found Him they fell down at His feet in adoration and surrender, presenting themselves and their gifts to Him.

How wondrously grand the grace of God is! When God would give the superlatively beautiful prophecy of the Star-King Sceptre-bearing Messiah, he does not select an Abraham, an Aaron, a Moses or a Joshua, but a Gentile pagan diviner of questionable character. God's mighty Spirit comes upon a heathen seer, and makes him, at least for the time being, what he never was, a *bona fide* prophet of God, to utter one of the sublimest Messianic prophecies in the Old Testament.

When God would announce the birth of the King of kings, He does not bring the wealthy or noble of Jerusalem, or the educated or the Scribes and

Pharisees to the humble house in Bethlehem. Marvelous grace! Messiah's star again appears to Gentile eyes in far-distant lands. Guiding them over mountains, desert and river, they journey laboriously under the spell of a God-given star to the Word Incarnate cradled upon a virgin's breast.

While those who knew about Messiah's coming, and had every opportunity to welcome Him, would not journey the half-dozen miles from Jerusalem to Bethlehem to greet Him, strangers from the covenants and promises, and aliens from the household of God, traverse uncounted miles of inhospitable terrain to fall at the feet of Him Whom they recognize as "the Star out of Jacob" and "the Sceptre out of Israel." Oh, for a similar faith that will make us wise, like them, to discern the splendid glory and luminous loveliness of the Son of God and Savior of the world, and to seek Him until we find Him, and having found Him yield our all to Him in holy service and sacrifice.

> *There's a song in the air!*
> *There's a star in the sky!*
> *There's a mother's deep prayer,*
> *And a baby's low cry!*
> *And the star rains its fire*
> *While the beautiful sing,*
> *For the manger in Bethlehem*
> *Cradles a King!*
>
> *There's a tumult of joy*
> *O'er the wonderful birth,*
> *For the Virgin's sweet Boy*
> *Is the Lord of the earth.*
> *Ay! the star rains its fire*

While the beautiful sing,
For the manger of Bethlehem
Cradles a King!

In the light of the star
Lie the ages impearled,
And the song from afar
Has swept over the world.
Every heart is aflame,
And the beautiful sing,
In the homes of the nations
That Jesus is King!

We rejoice in the light,
And we echo the song
That comes down through the night
From the heavenly throng.
Ay! we shout to the lovely
Evangel they bring,
And we greet in His cradle
Our Savior and King!

Josiah G. Holland

DAWN AND THE DAY STAR

And we have the word of prophecy made more sure;
whereunto ye do well that ye take heed, as unto a
lamp shining in a dark place, until the day dawn,
and the day star arise in your hearts (2 Pet. 1:19).

Sin introduced darkness into the universe. Man's fall plunged the human race into spiritual and moral night. The earth, too, as man's abode, very soon afterwards became the scene of hatred, pride, murder, and the habitation of cruelty. The first man born of woman was a murderer, and his descendants were notorious for arrogance and sin. By the time of the Flood "the wickedness of man was great in the earth and . . . every imagination of the thoughts of his heart was only evil continually" (Gen. 6:5). Moreover, "the earth was corrupt before God and . . . filled with violence" (Gen. 6:11).

After the revelation of God's light and truth to Noah and his family in the midst of the almost universal darkness of sin, the human race soon degenerated again and man's rebellion was judged in the confusion of languages at Babel. Later Abraham and his posterity were called out of idolatry to serve the one true God. But woeful defection characterized even his descendants and their unbelief culminated in putting to death their very Messiah Himself when, in the fulness of time, He came.

The Christian centuries also have been a period of great darkness, despite widespread gospel light. Frequently the Scripture refers to the present evil world as darkness. The Apostle Paul, for example, says believers "are not of the night, nor darkness" (1 Thess. 5:5), and that they "are seen as lights in the world" in the midst of "a crooked and perverse generation" (Phil. 2:15).

Both the incarnate Word and the written Word are described in terms of light. Thus the Apostle John says of the Word Incarnate: "In Him was life; and the life was the light of men. And the light shineth in the darkness; and the darkness apprehended it not" (John 1:4, 5). Jesus Himself said, "I am the light of the world: he that followeth me shall not walk in darkness, but shall have the light of life" (John 8:12).

Of the Written Word the Psalmist declares, "Thy word is a lamp unto my feet, and light unto my path" (Psa. 119:105). The writer of the Proverbs says, "For the commandment is a lamp; and the law is light" (Prov. 6:23). The Apostle Peter refers to the Word of God as Light and likens, especially the prophetic portions, to "a lamp shining in a dark place, until the day dawn, and the day star arise" in our hearts (2 Pet. 1:19).

A Dazzling Vision of Light

Peter and the other disciples were slow to learn the lessons our Lord endeavored to teach them. Although they were called out of the world, much of the darkness and spiritual ignorance of the world clung to their minds, even after they had basked in the light of the Messiah's wonderful person and teaching for a long time. Particularly gross was the darkness that engulfed their understanding with regard to prophetic truths. Christ's death and resurrection were wholly incomprehensible to them, as well as His ascension and glorious coming again.

To relieve the disciples' deep ignorance of things to come, especially of the divine future program as it hinged upon His death, our Lord presented to the three most spiritually apperceptive of his followers, a never-to-be-forgotten object lesson, now commonly referred to as the transfiguration. This audio-visual demonstration in the form of a mountain-top vision was a striking presentation of "the Son of man coming in his kingdom" (Matt. 16:28). It was calculated to arouse the spiritually dulled senses of the disciples and instruct them in "the sufferings of Christ and the glories that should follow" (1 Pet. 1:11).

As Peter, James and John were conducted "up into a high mountain apart" and Jesus "was transfigured before them," they came face to face with the overpowering splendor of Him "who is the blessed and only Potentate, the King of kings, and Lord of lords; who only hath immortality dwelling in light unapproachable" (1 Tim. 6:16). As Jesus was changed and as the glory of His deity began to shine through the veil of His human body of humiliation, "his face did shine as the sun, and his garments became white as the light" (Matt. 17:2).

In the midst of this scene of indescribably brilliant glory a notable feature became apparent. "And behold, there appeared unto them Moses and Elijah talking with him" (Matt. 17:3). Luke adds the tremendously significant statement that these Old Testament saints, representative of the law and the prophets, "appeared in glory" with Jesus and were discussing "his decease which he was about to accomplish at Jerusalem" (Luke 9:31). This is the explanation of the transcendant splendor of the transfiguration scene. The cross was the road to the crown. Suffering was to be the prelude to the magnificence of the kingdom. The first advent in shame and rejection must precede the second advent in triumph and glory.

The transfiguration as a portrayal of "the Son of man coming in his kingdom" contains in miniature all the elements of the future millennial rule of Christ in manifestation. The Lord Jesus is seen, not in humiliation, nor yet as "the day star," precursor of the dawn, but in radiant glory, with his face shining "as the sun" (Matt. 17:2), in full millennial splendor.

Moses, who died a natural death and was buried, is seen glorified and represents the redeemed who have passed through death into the kingdom (Luke 9:31). Elijah, the fiery prophet of Israel's decadent day, who was taken to heaven in a celestial chariot without dying, stands for the redeemed who have entered the kingdom by translation (1 Cor. 15:50-53; 1 Thess. 4:13-17).

Peter, James and John, not glorified, but appearing as men in the flesh in the scope of the vision, represent Israelites in the flesh in the future kingdom (Ezek. 37:21-27). The multitude of needy people whom Peter, James and John encountered when they came down from the mountain (Matt. 17:14) are representative of the nations in the flesh who are to be conducted into the kingdom after it is established over Israel (Isa. 11:10-12; Zech. 8:20-23).

Many years later as Peter was writing his second epistle, he employs his experience on the Mount of transfiguration as corroborating evidence of the truthfulness of his teaching on prophecy and the second advent of Christ in glory.

"For we did not follow cunningly devised fables, when we made known unto you the power and coming of our Lord Jesus Christ, but we were eyewitnesses of his majesty. For he received from God the Father honor and glory, when there was borne such a voice to him by the Majestic Glory, This is my beloved Son in

Whom I am well pleased: and the voice we ourselves heard borne out of heaven, when we were with him in the holy mount" (2 Pet. 1:16-18).

A Lamp in a Dark Place

The transfiguration of Jesus "in the holy mount" was like a blazing meteor bursting forth with sudden brilliance and illuminating the radiant glory of Christ in His coming kingdom. But it was soon past, and the disciples before long found the magnificence of the mountain-top experience had failed as they once more faced the darkness and ignorance of sin-stricken and suffering humanity at the foot of the mountain.

Even at the climax of Christ's transfigured glory "there came a cloud and overshadowed" the disciples, "and they feared as they entered into the cloud" (Luke 9:34). Their sin-dulled eyes could not then bear such a manifestation of effulgent light, and it was partially being hidden from them. Only as they apprehended and appropriated the meaning of Christ's death as it would eventuate in His resurrection, ascension and glorious coming again would their spiritual eyes become accustomed to such a blaze of revealed glory. But long years of instruction, suffering and discipline, and in many cases martyrdom, would be necessary to prepare them in the fullest sense for this.

Meanwhile, God had for them and for us in our common sinfulness and weakness a lesser light—bright, but not too bright to dazzle our frail vision, but sufficiently luminous to show us the pathway ahead, step by step, stop by stop, guiding us unerringly through the sin-obscured dark till the rise of the day star and the break of dawn. Of this divinely provided lantern Peter says: "And we have *the word of prophecy* made more sure; whereunto ye do well that ye take heed, *as unto a lamp shining in a dark place,* until the day dawn, and the day star arise in your hearts" (2 Pet. 1:19).

The lamp, then, is the sure and certain Word of God. To the man who will take it in his hand and hide it in his heart, it will shine with a soft and steady lustre, disclosing stumbling block and treacherous snare, revealing the dangerous precipice and every hidden peril.

But the Apostle Peter is thinking particularly of the Word of God in its prophetic or predictive aspect. "And we have the word of prophecy" says he, or more literally, "the prophetic word." For him this involved the great prophecies of the Old Testament centering in the first and second advents of Christ. Since the first advent with its far-reaching prophecies was a fulfilled event, the Apostle has principally in mind the second coming of Christ, with the vast prophetic panorama that surrounds this climactic event of the ages.

This "prophetic word . . . as a lamp shining in a dark place" is the lantern God has given His pilgrim-sojourners to conduct them through the darkness of this world until the dawning of the new age. This divinely provided light-giver sheds its dark-dispelling rays not only immediately around the pilgrim's feet showing him the next step ahead, but it casts its penetrating gleam far into the night, disclosing to the wayfarer also the general character of the world about him and furnishing a definite idea of the nature of the path ahead, as well as the destination to which it leads.

This prophetic word, guiding through the dark so wondrously as a lamp, the Apostle declares was "made more sure" or corroborated by the experience he and his colleagues James and John had in witnessing the transfiguration of Christ on "the holy mount." So resplendent and magnificent had that experience been that it had made an ineradicable impression on the rugged fisherman-Apostle, which the passing years could not erase.

Peter now remembers the dazzling display of glory and the grandeur of that divinely given object lesson in prophecy. As he does so, he contrasts it with the lesser light of the prophetic portions of the inspired Word of God, accommodated as it is in its softer gleam to pilgrim eyes and much more practical in its unfluctuating and constant shining in conducting the child of God through the journey of the night till the break of dawn.

DAY DAWNING

The Apostle Peter sees the second coming of Christ in glory as the dawning of day after the darkness of night. The pre-advent period of world history is represented as "night" because morally and spiritually this was true. The world now is the place "where Satan's throne is" (Rev. 2:13) and where he, through the agency of wicked men, has to a large measure taken over control, and where many temptations and pitfalls face the believer. Consequently, since the Christian must journey on his way to heaven through this sin-filled perilous night, the Apostle declares most solemnly that those "do well" who "take heed" to the prophetic word, gleaming like a lamp "in a dark place."

The Apostle's expression "dark place," aptly characterizes this Satan-dominated sphere. Behind the word "dark" there is the etymological idea of "dry" or "parched" which the world is spiritually, then "squalid" which the world is morally. Into this "murky realm" the prophetic word shines like a lamp to guide God-seeking souls till Christ returns to dispel the darkness and usher in millennial day.

The present age and all previous ages since the fall have constituted the night. Since man fell into sin, the prophetic word pointing toward the Coming Redeemer has been the constant never-failing light shining upon the path of the child of God.

"The true light" that "lighteth every man that cometh into the world" (John 1:5) appeared in Jesus Christ of Nazareth. But He was rejected by His own generation and nailed to a cross. The vast majority of people in the world have refused the light and have gone on in darkness. But wherever the lamp of the Word is followed, Christ, the Light, is received and enters the heart to illuminate the life of the believer. But believers, although "light in the Lord" (Eph. 5:8), and shining "as lights in the world, holding forth the Word of life" (Phil. 2:15, 16), nevertheless live in the midst of the darkness of this age.

The darkness, moreover, will continue until Christ returns in glory. When at last the heavens open and the White-horse Rider whose name is "Faithful and

True," whose "eyes are a flame of fire" and upon whose head "are many diadems" (Rev. 19:11, 12) descends to earth with terrible majesty and indescribable glory, darkness will flee away. Sin and ungodliness will at last be put down as He that "hath on his garments a name written, King of kings and Lord of lords" (Rev. 19:16) slays His enemies and in absolute righteousness rules the nations with a rod of iron.

When this great earth-shaking event toward which all history is moving takes place, the entire world will see the glory of the Son of Man as Peter, James and John saw it on the Mount of transfiguration. Then the resplendent kingdom of Christ, manifested in miniature to the disciples of old, will be revealed to every kindred, tongue and nation in all its world-wide sweep and grandeur. Then "the earth shall be full of the knowledge of Jehovah, as the waters cover the sea" (Isa. 11:9) and every mountain will be "a holy mount" of transfiguration (2 Pet. 1:18), and every valley and plain as well.

Then glorified saints, represented by Moses and Elijah, together with the nation Israel and the Gentile nations in the flesh, will intermingle freely as earth and heaven come into closer proximity, prefigured by Jacob's ladder set up on the earth and reaching to heaven, "and the angels of God ascending and descending upon the Son of Man" (Gen. 28:12; John 1:51). This bright age will mark the dawn of the millennial day, when "the sun of righteousness" arises "with healing in its beams" (Mal. 4:2).

DAWN AND THE DAY STAR

In exhorting his readers to take heed unto "the word of prophecy . . . as unto a lamp shining in a dark place," Peter emphasizes that this is to be done "till the day dawn and the day star arise" (2 Pet. 1:19). By "the day star" the Apostle means the Lord Jesus, Whom John the Revelator calls "the bright, the morning star" (Rev. 22:16).

The symbolic designation of our Lord as "the day star" or "the morning star" is exquisite. As the eastern sky begins to brighten toward dawn, the last planets to rise before their shining is lost in the increasing light of day were called "morning stars." As the final luminaries to appear in the East before sunrise, they are the heralds of the sunrise.

The morning stars thus belong to the night, but point to the coming of the day. In the broader sense the morning stars are the planets that have their rise after midnight whereas evening stars are those that appear from dusk till midnight. Moreover, the morning stars, like evening stars, are brilliant because as planets they have no light or heat of their own as stars do, but reflect the light of the sun, much like a mirror.

The most brilliant of all the planetary bodies is Venus, which has its orbit between Mercury and the Earth. It was both a morning and an evening star, depending on its alternate appearance. It was thus styled both Lucifer, the morning star, and Hesperus, the evening star, by the ancients.

The clear radiant lustre of the planet Venus, so

resplendent against the blackness of the nocturnal skies, is a superlatively beautiful symbol of the Lord Jesus Christ, Who in the night-time of this dispensation shines with splendor in the hearts of His own and is revealed to them in all His radiant loveliness against the somber background of the world's sin.

It was this supernal splendor of the preincarnate Christ, the Eternal Word, shining so radiantly in the sin-free pristine ages of eternity past, that Lucifer, himself a dazzling "day-star, son of the morning" (Isa. 14:12), coveted. Unsatisfied with the highest station of any creature, he determined to usurp the incomparable glory of the Creator Himself. This unholy purpose to be "like the Most High" corrupted His beauty, and transformed the radiant Anointed Cherub into a deadly enemy of the true "bright and morning star" and of all who love Him and worship His all-glorious Person.

But as "the bright, the morning star" our Lord does not appear to sinners or worldlings. They are asleep. As the Apostle Paul says, "They that sleep, sleep in the night; and they that are drunken are drunken in the night" (1 Thess. 5:7). Since we "are all sons of light, and sons of the day" and "not of the night or of darkness," we are not to "sleep as do the rest," but "watch and be sober" (1 Thess. 5:5, 6).

Only those who love our Lord sincerely, serve Him faithfully and eagerly watch for His coming, glimpse Him in the special morning-star beauty and radiance with which He is revealed to loving hearts who are vigilant and sober, and who longingly wait for His coming to receive them unto Himself (John 14:3). To them, His blood-bought church, He will arise as the "day star," "the bright, the morning star" calling them unto Himself before the light of the millennial dawn breaks.

It is significant that the term "the bright, the morning star" is used by our Lord concerning Himself. The fact also that it is employed in His final testimony in the last book of the Bible and the last chapter of that book, gives it a unique solemnity. The language in which He utters it, and the other appellations He couples with it, give it additional emphasis: *"I Jesus have sent mine angel to testify unto you these things for the churches. I am the root and the offspring of David, the bright, the morning star* (Rev. 22:16).

Our Lord's designation of Himself as "the root and the offspring of David" speaks of Him as the divine-human King over Israel. As divine He is the *Root* or Originator of David's line. As human He is the *Offspring* or Descendant of David. He is both David's Lord and David's son (Psa. 110:1). The crown of Israel is His by virtue of Who He is, and His, too, by promise and prophecy. He was born "King of the Jews" (Matt. 2:2). He died "King of the Jews" (Matt. 27:37). He shall yet "restore the kingdom to Israel" (Acts 1:6) and reign as King of the Jews (Zech. 9:9) when the millennial morn breaks.

But before the manifested glory of the millennial age, Jesus appears as "the bright, the morning star" to His Bride, the church. The star rises in the early morning and precedes the shining of the sun. So Christ will appear to His own in the lustre of the morning star to take them to Himself before the darkest part of the night—the tribulation period—precedes the dawn.

As soon as our Blessed Lord announces Himself as "the bright, and the morning star," the Spirit resident in the church upon the earth cries out to the Lord, "Come!" And the church, the Bride at once aroused by the voice of her beloved, also cries out "Come!" It is a cry of Christ's own for His coming as "the bright, and the morning star."

Then the Apostle John by the Spirit urges him "that heareth" to say "Come!" as he himself says in closing the Revelation: "He who testifieth these things saith, Yes, I come quickly. *Amen: come, Lord Jesus* (Rev. 22:20).

Meanwhile, the general invitation goes out to him "that is athirst," to come. But the exhortation here is not directed to the soon-returning Christ, but to the thirsty soul to come "take the water of life freely," that in turn, with his soul-thirst quenched in Christ, he might say with the Spirit and the Bride and with him that heareth and the Apostle John himself, *"Amen, come, Lord Jesus."*

God grant that the radiant glory of our blessed Lord as "the bright, the morning star" may so shine into our hearts and captivate our affections, that our heart-cry may ever be, till we see His blessed face and the prints of the nails in His hands, *"Amen, come, Lord Jesus."*

There's a light upon the mountain,
  And the day is at the spring,
When our eyes shall see the beauty
  And the glory of the King:
Weary was our heart with waiting,
  And the night watch seemed so long,
But His triumph-day is breaking,
  And we hail it with a song.

In the fading of the starlight
  We may see the coming morn;
And the lights of men are paling
  In the splendors of the dawn:
For the eastern skies are glowing
  As with light of hidden fire,
And the hearts of men are stirring
  With the throbs of deep desire.
                              Henry Burton

Help us gaze upon Thy splendor,
  Bright and Morning Star so fair,
For our hope is, gracious Savior,
  To be caught up in the air.
Let Thy glory in the night sky,
  Blessed Harbinger of day
Kindle holy expectation;
  "Come, Lord Jesus Christ," we pray.
                              Merrill F. Unger

STARLIT PATH TO GLORY

Chapter Seven

They Shall Shine As the Stars

And they that are wise shall shine as the brightness of the firmament; and they that turn many to righteousness as the stars forever and ever
                                        (Dan. 12:3).

DARKNESS AND STAR-LIKE SAINTS

. . . I saw seven golden candlesticks, and in the midst of the candlesticks one like unto the son of man . . . And he had in his right hand seven stars . . .
(Rev. 1:13, 16).

God has a definite purpose in having allowed sin and darkness to invade His universe. No doubt finite minds, themselves darkened by sin, will never be able to comprehend the complete answer to all the problems connected with the divine permission of sin, at least this side of heaven. Nevertheless, the salient points stand out clearly in the thinking of the believer, who is willing to rest his faith in the testimony of the Scriptures and repose his confidence in the infinite grace and goodness of God.

Certainly if there had been no sin, there could have been so salvation. If there had been no salvation, there could never have been a Savior. Had there been no Savior, there could never have been the magnificent manifestation of God's grace and love centering in the incarnation and the cross. In such a case think how immeasurably impoverished would be our understanding of the inmost heart of God.

Again, had there been no sin, there would have been no trial, suffering or conflict. Without these, how deficient would our Christian character be! Without trial how could our faith be proved genuine?

Without suffering, how could we know the tenderness and compassion of Christ? Without conflict how could there be the joy of conquest and the thrill of achievement?

If there had been no sin, there would have been no darkness. If there were no darkness, how could we really appreciate the light? If there were no night, would we not miss the splendor of the nocturnal skies and the loveliness of the stars? If there were no sin, how could there be star-like saints? Surely, one great purpose of God in allowing sin to invade His sinless universe is to display the marvels of His grace manifested in His saints as that grace is magnified against the sombre background of sin and its misery.

The Apostle Paul emphasizes this transcendent and eternal purpose of God when he says: "that in the ages to come he might show the exceeding riches of his grace in kindness toward us in Christ Jesus" (Eph. 2:7).

STAR-LIKE SAINTS AND SIN-DARKENED NIGHT

The Apostle Paul in describing true believers in the world uses the lovely image of the star-studded night heavens. Certainly the great Apostle, like most of us, often had the experience of gazing into the luminous expanse of the firmament on a cloudless night. The brilliant and sparkling array of celestial luminaries that caught his eye and led him to awed worship and praise, also reminded him of God's saints in this world of sin. The black heavens spoke to him of this present godless age and he saw in each shining star, giving forth a clear and constant light, a graphic picture of a child of God rising star-like on the night of surrounding evil.

In writing to his beloved Philippian converts the Apostle uses the figure of nocturnal luminaries in his tender pleading with them to live as Christ's own ought to live. "So then, my beloved," says he, "even as ye have always obeyed . . . work out your own salvation with fear and trembling; for it is God Who worketh in you both to will and to work, for his good pleasure. Do all things without murmurings and questionings; that ye may become blameless and harmless, children of God without blemish in the midst of a crooked and perverse generation, *among whom ye are seen as lights in the world*" (Phil. 2:14-16).

The Apostle mentions three ways the Philippians were to exhibit their normal star-like character as those redeemed by the blood of Christ, indwelt by the Holy Spirit and clothed with the light and beauty of their Redeemer's holiness. First, they were "to work out" their own salvation. Secondly, they were to do all things without complainings and criticisms. Thirdly, they were to hold forth the Word of life to the unsaved.

Working out our own salvation is most vitally connected with a star-like experience. This injunction has often been misunderstood and belabored with a legalistic interpretation. But the Apostle is most emphatically *not* speaking of working for salvation, but of working it out. And what a world of difference! God alone can work it *in* purely by His grace in response to our faith in the finished work of Christ (Eph. 2:8, 9). We alone can work it *out* by realizing what Christ accomplished for us on the cross and *acting* on the basis of that accomplishment.

The question, therefore, of vital import is, *What did Christ accomplish for us on the cross?* In briefest statement, it may be said, He gave us an entirely new position of vital organic union with Himself in death, burial, and resurrection (Gal. 2:20), so that *every believer* is "in Christ" (Rom. 6:3, 4). Sharing Christ's death cuts us off from our "sin-death" position "in Adam." Sharing Christ's burial puts away the old life of sin. Participating in Christ's resurrection gives us the divine power essential to live out our new "righteousness-life" position "in Christ."

Comprehending our *position* and *acting in faith* upon it, translates *position in Christ* into a moment-by-moment *experience of Christ* (Rom. 6:11). This translation of our *position,* which is perfect because we are "in Christ," Who is perfect (Col. 2:9, 10) into *concrete experience* which, however, is perfect only in proportion as it is reckoned upon by faith, is shining for Christ and maintaining a star-like testimony in this scene of darkness and sin. When believers see *what they are in Christ* (*not* what they are in themselves), Christ as "the light of the world" begins to shine through them and be reflected from them, making them "appear as lights" in the midst of "a crooked and perverse generation."

The second way believers are to shine as luminaries in the sin-gloom of this age is to "do all things without murmurings and questionings" (Phil. 2:14). Nothing so readily tarnishes our testimony as a dissatisfied and complaining spirit or an attitude of captious criticism. This was one of the blighting sins of Israel in the wilderness and has always been a major detriment to the progress of God's work in every age. God's people bring reproach upon the gospel and cause our Lord's name to be blasphemed by unbelievers when murmuring and discord blur the star-like witness a Christian ought to have in a sin-darkened world.

The third way believers are to shine as stars is by "holding forth the Word of life" (Phil. 2:16). Soul-winning endeavor either on the part of the local church or the individual believer is a panacea for spiritual ills, such as criticisms, divisions, carnality, worldliness, murmurings and the inevitable frustration of self-occupation.

Taking the gospel to the lost works a double blessing—upon the one who carries the message and upon the one who receives the message. One in "holding forth the Word of life" enjoys the tonic and preventive effects of being busy for God and for others. The other in receiving "the Word of life" becomes the beneficiary of the spiritual healing and eternal life it brings.

Both he who holds forth the Word of life and he who accepts its message receive light. The soul-winner radiates the light of Christ and the soul that is won embraces "the light of the gospel of the glory of Christ," which "dawns" upon him (2 Cor. 4:4).

Thus in working out their inwrought salvation, in doing "all things without murmurings and questionings" and in "holding forth the Word of life" the saints at Philippi were to "become blameless and harmless, children of God without rebuke *in the midst* of a crooked and perverse generation" among whom they were to appear "as lights in the world" (Phil. 2:15, 16) .

"Blameless and harmless, the children of God without rebuke" is the Apostle Paul's definition of a star-like saint. That such a Christian, radiating the light of his Savior and Lord, might not hastily conclude that such a glowing experience demands withdrawal from a sinful world and cloistered isolation, the Apostle quickly adds that a believer is to maintain such a shining testimony *"in the midst of"* this sin-blighted age, which he aptly describes as "a crooked and perverse generation."

How wonderful a picture of the dignity and the superlative ministry of a Christian in this evil world—to shine as stars! *As the stars?* How bright and glorious they are! How clear, brilliant and sparkling! What an encouragement to the child of God in his pilgrimage through the world to know that however difficult his way may be, however beset by oppositions and sufferings, in his witness he is compared to the stars.

As the undimmed splendor of the stars shines out in the blackness of the surrounding night, so the Christian's testimony is to radiate the glory of His Lord, "the true light . . . which lighteth every man coming into the world" (John 1:9) . As the deepening shadows of advancing evening only increase the brilliance of the starry host above, so may the star-like saint rejoice to know that his own witness is increased in its lustre as the darkness of the age deepens. Let his joy be full as he considers that He Who said "I am the Light of the world" (John 8:12) also declared, "Ye are the light of the world" (Matt. 5:14). What an inestimable privilege to "show forth the excellencies of him" Who called us "out of darkness into his marvellous light" (1 Peter 2:9). May we ever be diligent in doing this by maintaining a star-like testimony.

STARS IN CHRIST'S RIGHT HAND

The introductory vision of the Apocalyptic seer, John, in the book of the Revelation presents an awesome scene in which the glorified Lord Jesus Christ appears in splendid dignity, as a Priest-Judge. Invested with the august robes of magisterial power, the great Adjudicator is envisioned in the role which He conspicuously plays throughout the vast judgment scenes of the end-time preceding His second coming.

The immediate context, however, is that of judgment upon His church (Rev. 1:10-3:22). "For the time is come for judgment to begin at the house of God: and if it begin first at us, what shall be the end of them that obey not the gospel of God?" (1 Pet. 4:17).

Because the setting is that of darkness and night, the vision flashes with added splendor against the somber background. Stars and candlesticks, or lampstands, are seen, which belong to the night, and suggest the moral and spiritual gloom of the age.

The appearance of the glorified Son of Man scintillating with dazzling light against the darkness of night, recalls the splendor of the transfiguration scene, which the Apostle John had witnessed many years previously. The seer was "in the Spirit on the Lord's day" (Rev. 1:10). By this expression he evidently means that he was under a special prophetic inspiration that transported Him by means of the Holy Spirit into the future day of the Lord and the events leading up to this apocalyptic period.

Looking behind him, the Apostle hears a trumpet-like voice bidding him write what is being said and send the message to seven then-existing churches in the province of Asia. Turning to see whence the voice came, John was presented with the greatest sight human eyes can ever behold—a vision of the glorified Son of Man.

Attired in long judicial robes reaching "down to the foot", and girt about the breasts with a golden girdle" (Rev. 1:13), speaking of His character as judge, our Lord is presented in such overpowering splendor that when John saw Him he "fell at his feet as one dead" (Rev. 1:17).

Christ's "head and his hair were white as white wool, white as snow," recalling Daniel's vision of the "ancient of days" (Dan. 7:9). "His eyes were as a flame of fire; and his feet like unto burnished brass, as if it had been refined in a furnace" (Rev. 1:14, 15). Those eyes that had tenderly wept at the grave of Lazarus, here burn with omniscient fire, and those feet that walked the Via Dolorosa of human suffering and were pierced with nails, now resemble incandescent brass and soon tread "the winepress of the fierceness of the wrath of God, the Almighty" (Rev. 19:15), tramping Satan, Antichrist and wicked earth-dwellers under foot.

"His voice as the voice of many waters" is infinitely

grand and thunderously majestic, but fearfully terrifying to the sinner as the Judge passes sentence: "Depart from me, ye cursed, into the eternal fire, which is prepared for the devil and his angels" (Matt. 25:41).

"Out of his mouth proceedeth a sharp two-edged sword." This is the "sword of justice," the word of judgment, pronounced by the gloriously returning Christ upon His enemies and sinners, which shall be immediate and irremediable in its terrible effect. "His countenance . . . as the sun shineth in its strength" describes the Lord's awful majesty as "the sun of righteousness" (Mal. 4:2) rising with healing in His beams to dispel the darkness of the end of this age and inaugurate the resplendent millennial day.

Two features of this dazzling vision of light, however, connect it with a background of darkness. The Son of Man in His glory is "in the midst of . . . candlesticks" or lampstands (Rev. 1:13) and he has "in his right hand seven stars" (Rev. 1:16). The "stars" and the "lampstands," which give light at night, plainly point to the darkness of the present dispensation of the church while our Lord is away.

The Mystery of the Seven Stars

The stars in the right hand of the Son of Man and the lampstands among which He walks are the only details of the vision that are presented as needing interpretation. It is, moreover, singular that these are the elements of the prophetic symbolism that place John's vision in the darkness of the present age.

Both the stars and lampstands are said to be a "mystery" (Rev. 1:20). This expression does not denote that which is beyond our understanding but simply that which must be *revealed* to be comprehended. Actually, it refers to a truth heretofore hidden; but now made known, but whose meaning may still be veiled under a symbol.

The symbols of the stars and lampstands are accordingly revealed to be "angels" and "churches." "The seven stars are the angels of the seven churches and the seven candlesticks (lampstands) are seven churches" (Rev. 1:20).

The stars, symbolizing "angels," denote the ministers or messengers to the seven churches, appointed by the Lord and responsible to Him for the spiritual condition of each assembly. They are styled "angels of the churches" because they are divinely sent to the assemblies to guard them and to represent them.

Such ministers may or may not receive men's recognition, but they deal with the Lord directly concerning the assembly which each represents. They are capable of receiving personal communications from Christ regarding the welfare of the assembly and are answerable to Him for carrying them out.

That these ministers or messengers to the churches, as stars, are held in the right hand of Christ (Rev. 2:1) presents an exceedingly beautiful and instructive picture. It teaches that God's true ministers being viewed by him as "stars," as such have the responsibility to shine. Doubtless the planets are meant, since these do not shine of themselves by the combustion of any gaseous elements in their composition as do ordinary stars, but are luminous because they reflect light from the sun.

Christian ministers have no light of their own, but simply reflect the light of Christ. This is their beauty, as well as their duty, and this alone warrants their being dignified by our Lord Himself as "stars." But our Lord not only honors them as "stars," but as such holds them in His "right hand," the place of supreme authority and honor (Psa. 110:1; Eph. 1:20; Rev. 5:1, 7). What a responsible, yet at the same time honorable, position every minister in the church occupies!

What a position of security also is enjoyed by every true representative of Christ! Held in the right hand of the Son of God! If Christ's ministers are true to their responsibility as stars to shine, who can pluck them out of His protecting hand or do them harm, save that which He allows? If they are untrue to their trust and fail to shine, how shall they escape from Him Who holds them in His omnipotent grasp?

No figure could be more eloquently expressive of our Lord's competency to give or withhold, to preserve and tenderly sustain every true minister of His, than the portrait of the Son of God with seven stars in His right hand.

But the Christian who is not formally a "minister" is not to be deprived of the wonderful comfort afforded by the blessed truth that our Lord holds the seven stars in His right hand. In a definite sense *all Christians are stars*, since all are His representatives, *all* are His servants, and *all* are to shine for Him.

Moreover, *all* Christians have an interest in the assembly, and *all* may receive communication from Him concerning its welfare and are responsible to carry out His injunctions. All, too, are held in the right hand of the Son of God and in the fullest, most assuring sense are supported and sustained lovingly by Him in their light-bearing ministry.

THE MYSTERY OF THE SEVEN GOLDEN LAMPSTANDS

The seven golden lampstands are revealed to be "seven churches." Again the scene is night, for lampstands are the bearers of light to illuminate the darkness. It is important to see that the lampstand is not the light. The light is the Lord's, not the church's. From Him it receives the light and sends forth its rays to a sin-darkened world.

Churches are but the aggregate of individual Christians. Since individual believers "are seen as lights in the world" (Phil. 2:15), the church is likewise to appear as a light-bearer and light-dispenser "in the midst of a crooked and perverse generation."

The lampstands, moreover, are of gold. This most precious metal speaks of the deity of Christ and the divine righteousness. The church being founded on the rock of our Lord's deity (Matt. 16:18) is called to proclaim God's righteousness and how the crucified and risen Savior has provided the way for sinners to meet its demands and obtain salvation.

The "seven" lampstands speak of the church as a whole, although set forth as separate assemblies. The "seven" also signifies the church's completion and perfection on earth as Christ's light-bearer, not viewed as what the church has become, but seen in its origin and character as founded by our divine Lord Himself.

Indeed, the Son of Man appears "in the midst of the lampstands" (Rev. 1:13) in most precious intimacy and with infinite love and concern for their good. Nevertheless, His attitude is that of the Priest-Judge, rather than that of the Intercessor. In fact, He is judging each church's *use of the light* and dealing with each assembly on the basis of *its responsibility to burn brightly*! For as lampstands bearing light, they are entitled to the oil of the Holy Spirit and to Christ as the Light. Moreover, the night is dark and desperately needs their clear, brightly shining testimony.

How glorious is God's intention for His redeemed people in a somber world of sin! All His saints are "lights" or luminaries to shine for His glory in a morally and spiritually darkened age (Phil 2:14, 15). His ministers and special representatives are bright "stars," held securely in the right hand of the Son of Man, witnessing for Christ in the church as the stars do in the terrestrial heavens (Rev. 1:20). His churches, moreover, are "golden lampstands," proclaiming His deity and Saviorhood, bearing the oil of the precious Holy Spirit and shedding forth His glory.

"Lights," "stars" and "lampstands" are for the night and dark places. God's purpose for us in constituting us "lights," "stars" and "lamps" is that we may shine for Him. May He help us to see our dignity as "sons of light" and "sons of the day" (1 Thess. 5:5), and may we give forth such a steady unswerving gleam, piercing the pall of night, that no pilgrim journeying toward the celestial city will miss the way because we failed to shine for our blessed Redeemer.

> *Jesus is standing*
> *All-glorious in beauty,*
> *Garbed as a Judge,*
>   *Who is "Faithful and True."*
> *See in His right hand*
> *The stars He is holding!*
> *Christian, O Christian,*
>   *They represent you.*
>
> *Jesus is walking*
> *Amid golden lampstands,*
> *Darkness has fallen,*
>   *He's looking for light.*
> *Stir from thy slumber,*
> *O Church of the Firstborn,*
> *Calling, He's calling*
>   *For light in the night!*
>
> *When darkness gathers*
> *And sin round us presses,*
> *When shadows lengthen*
>   *And day turns to night,*
> *Awaken, O Christian,*
> *Shine for the Savior,*
> *Trim your lamp brightly*
>   *And shed forth your light.*
>
> *How beautiful to shine*
> *As the stars for the Savior!*
>   *Held in His right hand*
>   *Doing His blest command*
> *How beautiful to shine*
> *As the stars for the Savior*
>   *Led to Canaan's land.*
>   Merrill F. Unger

WHEN THE RIGHTEOUS SHINE AS THE STARS

Then shall the righteous shine forth as the sun in the kingdom of their Father (Matt. 13:43). *The wise shall shine as the brightness of the firmament . . . as the stars for ever and ever* (Dan. 12:3).

The blessing God has for His pilgrim people in this world, often in the midst of and in spite of their trials and sufferings, is immeasurable. Frequently the Father's faithful saints glimpse heaven before they arrive there and feel the glory of eternity in their souls during their most severe testings and temptations. It seems at times as if our gracious God is impatient to usher us into the glory that is awaiting us "in the land of light, where there is no night" and every now and then grants us a foretaste of it, as He did to the disciples on the Mount of Transfiguration with regard to the coming kingdom.

However, whatever glimpse of celestial bliss may be vouchsafed to us here in this vale of tears or whatever foretaste of heaven may be granted to buoy us up in times of special stress, these are nothing to be compared to the splendors of another world that shall dawn upon us when "this corruptible shall have put on incorruption, and this mortal shall have put on immorality" and this sin-freed, death-loosed, glorified body, liberated from the shackles of time and space cries exultingly, "O death, where is thy victory? O death where is thy sting?" (1 Cor. 15:54, 55).

This introduction to the glories of the heavenly realm will be thrilling to each redeemed heart, not merely because it will mean release from sin and death, but because it will signal the coming of the Deliverer Himself, the blessed Savior, to take His own unto Himself and accomplish in them all the benefits secured on Calvary's cross. "For the Lord Himself shall descend from heaven with a shout, with the voice of the archangel, and with the trump of God, and the dead in Christ shall rise first; then we that are alive that are left, shall together with them be caught up in the clouds to meet the Lord in the air: and so shall we ever be with the Lord" (1 Thess. 4:16, 17).

Then the Lord will be glorified in His own, as well as glorify and reward them for places of administration and authority in His coming Kingdom and His eternal program. From the human side and in holy anticipation of this "blessed hope" Christ's own may well sing the beloved hymn:

> *When He cometh, when He cometh*
> *To make up His jewels,*
> *All His jewels, precious jewels,*
> *His loved and his own.*
>
> *He will gather, He will gather*
> *The gems for His kingdom;*
> *All the pure ones, all the bright ones,*
> *His loved and His own.*
>
> *Little children, little children,*
> *Who love their Redeemer,*
> *Are the jewels, precious jewels,*
> *His loved and His own.*
>
> *Like the stars of the morning,*
> *His bright crown adorning,*

They shall shine in their beauty,
Bright gems for His crown.

W. O. Cushing

The Gift of the Morning Star

One of the most exquisite and far-reaching blessings the Lord bestows upon His faithful overcoming saints is an intense love for His appearing. This ardent adventism, manifested in a keen "looking for the blessed hope and appearing of the glory of the great God and our Savior Jesus Christ" (Titus 2:13), is in a very definite sense a reward given in time, but which extends blessedly into eternity.

Love for the Lord's return is a spiritual tonic reviving the weary heaven-bound pilgrim in his journey through the wilderness of this world, giving him strength to keep climbing the upward way. It will turn into a resplendent "crown of righteousness" (2 Tim. 4:8), placed upon the brow of the victorious saint in the day of the Lord's coming—a diadem that will radiate Christ's glory throughout the ages to come.

Love for Christ's appearing is a spiritual tonic because it indicates love for our Lord Himself—a love that sees in Him the One "altogether lovely" (Song 5:16), the "rose of Sharon" and the "lily of the valleys" (Song 2:1), a love that fastens its gaze upon the beauty of Christ and looks neither to the right hand nor left to be distracted by other loves.

Little wonder the Apostle John by inspiration describes such a pure lambent flame, burning out all the dross of lesser affections, consuming every idol, and purging out worldliness and selfishness, as a purifying "hope." "And every one that hath this hope set on him *purifieth himself,* even as he is pure" (1 John 3:3).

Little marvel this supreme love will be signally rewarded by Christ when He comes to receive His own and take them to the place He is preparing for them in His "Father's house" of "many mansions" (John 14:2). But such love is its own reward, even before Christ returns, and is mentioned in connection with the individual overcomer in the church of Thyatira, to whom our Lord says, *"I will give him the morning star"* (Rev. 2:28).

The church at Thyatira, the fourth of the seven churches of the Revelation, represents historically the "Dark Ages" of papal apostasy from the seventh century to the Reformation in the sixteenth century. No where in church history appears so unenlightened a period spiritually. All around was *night,* in the church and in the world.

A flood of worldliness, paganism and idolatry invaded the church, with veneration for the Virgin Mary and the worship of saints and images dethroning Christ from the place of sole supremacy. At the same time the church, more strictly the papacy, assumed the place of a spiritual dictator, and thereby rejected the supreme authority of the Word of God. This vast insweep of corruption continuing till "the deep things of Satan" (Rev. 2:24) were plumbed, is symbolized in the account in the Revelation under the figure of "Jezebel," reminiscent of Israel's idolatrous heathen queen, being permitted to teach abominations in the church (Rev. 2:20-24).

But side by side with this unprecedented darkness appeared a light—*the wondrous gleam of the morning star!* The superlative radiance of Christ, as the harbinger of the glorious coming day, was vouchsafed to those who triumphed over the paganistic error and idolatry that flooded the church of this period.

Nowhere in church history appears so intense a love for the person of Christ as in this grossly dark era. All around fell the awful pall of spiritual ignorance and idolatrous superstition. The threat of death hung like a Damoclean sword over any declaration of Bible truth. Notwithstanding, our Lord Himself granted to His victorious warriors *the rising day star in their hearts.*

The hope of the Lord's Coming was born in many tried and purified hearts. The promise of the risen and glorified Christ to each victor of this age rang out in the dark night: *"I will give him the morning star.*

In this dark night Christ was loved, served and celebrated in song. He was the only Light that pierced the awful darkness, when truth was burned at the stake and God's faithful prophets were done to death. But He was sufficient! And the hope of His coming— purifying, inspiring and sustaining as it was—made sufferings, persecutions and death endured by the faithful, bearable, yea, even glorious.

Many in the darkness of the dungeon had their eyes opened to see the celestial radiance of the ascending Morning Star. Many, as their physical eyes were put out, like Stephen, saw "the heavens opened, and the

Son of Man standing on the right hand of God" (Acts 7:56).

Many languishing in solitary confinement for the sake of the gospel, heard the wondrous words from the lips of the Lord Himself: ". . . That which ye have, hold fast till I come . . . He that overcometh, and he that keepeth my works unto the end, to him will I give authority over the nations: and he shall rule them with a rod of iron, as the vessels of a potter are broken to shivers; as I also received of my Father; *and I will give him the morning* star" (Rev. 2:25-28).

BELIEVERS' TESTIMONY AND STAR-GLORY

God's children, figuratively described as heavenly luminaries with respect to their light-bearing ministry amidst a dark world of sin, in many ways resemble the luminous beauty of the sidereal heavens. Whether in number, size, position or beauty, or whether as "lights" shining in the midst of "a crooked and perverse generation" (Phil. 2:15), or as specially lustrous planets held in the right hand of the Son of God (Rev. 1:16, 20), believers in a most beautifully expressive sense are like "stars." The analogy may be drawn out in detail with instruction and profit.

God's saints, for example, held securely in the right hand of the Son of God, resemble "fixed stars," shining with a "positioned" and steady glow. Or if planets are signified, they move (not "wander") in definite prescribed orbits, as good light-bearers for Christ serve only and always within the will of God.

On the other hand, false professors and unstable or apostate teachers, are completely unlike the stars that shine perpetually and unfailingly. Jude compares them to "wandering (Greek planetary) stars, for whom the blackness of darkness hath been reserved forever" (Jude 1:13). These are not our "planets" but either comets or meteors, more probably the latter, since meteors are aptly described as "falling stars."

Could any designation be more expressive of the inconstancy and unreliability of false professors and apostate teachers? Pyrotechnically they blaze like a comet, which is seen only for a few days or weeks at the most, and then is entirely lost sight of. Brilliantly, they flash out for a few moments, like a meteor, and then are totally extinguished.

The Apostle Paul in his discussion of the resurrection in the light of the glory of terrestrial and celestial bodies makes a definite reference to the varying glory of stellar bodies. "There is one glory of the sun, and another glory of the moon, *and another glory of the stars; for one star differeth from another star in glory* (1 Cor. 15:41).

This simple fact concerning the heavens alluded to incidentally by the Apostle, is now a well-known principle of astronomy. The stars are variously classified, first by their magnitudes or order of brightness. There are about twenty stars of the first magnitude, sixty-five of the second and two hundred of the third, et cetera, proceeding in geometric progression, so that of the sixth magnitude there are five thousand, of the tenth seven hundred and twenty thousand and so on. In a clear dark sky the average sixth magnitude star is the faintest visible to the naked eye.

More powerful telescopes are revealing stars of fainter and fainter lustre, which turn out to exist in prodigious profusion. The brightest star seen in all the heavens is Sirius, the dog star. It is twenty-seven times as bright as the sun. Other exceedingly luminous stars are Canopus, Vega, Capella, Arcturus, Rigel, Procyon and others.

An example of a great ball of brilliant luminaries is the globular cluster Omega Centauri. It contains at least 100,000 stars, numbers of them being bigger and brighter than the sun. It is one of the nearer clusters of this type, about 20,000 light years away. While resplendent Sirius is only nine light years distant.

Almost unimaginable differences exist in the brilliance of the stars. Great variations likewise exist in the effectiveness of the light-bearing testimony of believers. Some shine with a dazzling brilliance like Sirius, Canopus or Vega. Others gleam less penetratingly. Some are of far less magnitude. Many are so faint that their light cannot be seen with the unaided eye, but only under powerful telescopes.

There exist in addition to stars of varied brilliance dark or non-luminous stars. Many astronomers are of the opinion that these exceed the luminous stars in number. Be this as it may, they remind us of those who make a profession of being a Christian, but do not actually possess Christ, the light of the world, in their hearts.

Believers' Rewards and Star-Glory

Not only does Scripture compare the life and testimony of believers here in this present world to heavenly luminaries, but there are not lacking intimations that rewards and positions of glory in the world to come will also be of varied degrees of exaltation and eminence comparable to the diversified splendor of the stars. Daniel speaks of the faithful witnesses of the dark tribulation period as shining *"as the stars forever and ever"* (Dan. 12:3) which can scarcely be confined to a light-bearing ministry in this present life.

The Bible clearly reveals that there will be difference of rewards and honors assigned to believers in the life to come as a result of faithfulness in service in this earthly sphere after one has been saved. The Apostle Paul declares that *all* believers "must . . . be made manifest before the judgment-seat of Christ; that each one may receive the things done in the body, according to what he hath done, whether it be good or bad" (2 Cor. 5:10). In Romans 14:10 he also states that *all* Christians "shall . . . stand before the judgment seat of God."

In the First letter to the Corinthians the Apostle speaks at length of Christian rewards under the figure of constructing a building. The foundation is Christ. Christian service is building *on the foundation.* The kind of materials put into the building is either combustible ("wood, hay, stubble") or incombustible ("gold, silver, costly stones"). "The fire" which proves "each man's work of what sort it is" is Christ's all-probing evaluation of a Christian's life and testimony at the judgment of the Christian's works. "If any man's work shall abide which he built thereon, he shall *receive a reward.* If any man's work shall be burned, he shall suffer loss (i.e. of reward) ; yet himself shall be saved; yet so as through fire" (1 Cor. 3:10-15).

In another important passage on rewards the Apostle Paul gives two reasons why he bent every effort to serve Christ faithfully. The first was in order to win men to Christ (1 Cor. 9:19-23) and the second, as a means of securing *reward for approved service* (1 Cor. 9:24-27). To illustrate his point he uses the figures of foot-racing and boxing as practiced in the celebrated Isthmian games of ancient Greece.

Elsewhere in Scripture rewards are spoken of as *crowns*. "The crown of life" (Rev. 2:10) is the martyr's award. "The crown of glory" (1 Pet. 5:4) will be placed upon the brow of the faithful pastor. "The crown of rejoicing" is the diligent soul-winner's portion (1 Thess. 2:19; Phil. 4:1). "The crown incorruptible" (1 Cor. 9:27) will be awarded for temperance and self-control. "The crown of righteousness" is for those to whom the Lord gives "the morning star" (Rev. 2:28) and who love His "appearing" (2 Tim. 4:8).

What a wonderful prospect for the believer! Saved by grace through faith, God does not, and cannot, reckon the Christian's merit or work to the account of his salvation. But it is required that the believer's good works shall be divinely acknowledged, and God has fully provided for this necessity in the doctrine of rewards, which is an essential counterpart of the doctrine of salvation by grace.

The saved soul owes nothing to God in payment for salvation, which is granted purely as a gift (Eph.

2:8-10). But the believer does owe God a life of absolute devotion and service. For this expression of spontaneous gratitude, God promises rewards in heaven. These are indicated to be revealed to God's faithful ones and are:

"Things which eye saw not, and ear heard not
And which entered not into the heart of man,
Whatsoever things God prepared for them that love
  him."

(1 Cor. 2:9).

Elsewhere the Apostle refers to the grand prospect of future rewards for faithfulness as "an eternal weight of glory" (2 Cor. 4:17). He urges the Thessalonians to walk "worthily" of God, who "calleth you into his own kingdom and glory" (1 Thess. 2:12). The Apostle Peter speaks of partaking "of the glory that shall be revealed" (1 Pet. 5:1) and of being called unto "eternal glory in Christ" (1 Pet. 5:10).

Surely, God who has so graciously saved us has rewards for his faithful suffering children that will be indescribable. They shall shine "as the stars of the morning." Those that have endured suffering, privation, hardship "for the word of God and the testimony of Jesus" (Rev. 1:9), shall "shine forth as the sun in the kingdom of their Father" (Matt. 13:43), even as the Sun of Righteousness Himself, their exalted Lord, whom they loved and served so passionately in this life:

> Ten thousand times ten thousand
>   In sparkling raiment bright,
> The armies of the ransomed saints
>   Throng up the steeps of light:
> 'Tis finished, all is finished,

> *Their fight with death and sin:*
> *Fling open wide the golden gates,*
> *And let the victors in.*

> *What rush of alleluias*
> *Fill all the earth and sky!*
> *What ringing of a thousand harps*
> *Bespeaks the triumph nigh!*
> *O day, for which creation*
> *And all the tribes were made;*
> *O joy, for all its former woes*
> *A thousand times repaid.*
>   Henry Alford

Shining As the Stars Forever

The prophecy of Daniel contains a particularly beautiful reference to a yet-future period in the history of Israel when the nation will be blessed by a certain group of preeminent teachers and exemplars whom the prophet likens to stars. "And they that are wise shall shine as the brightness of the firmament; and they that turn many to righteousness as the stars forever and ever" (Dan. 12:3).

The hour is to be the darkest one in all the troubled history of the Jewish people. It is "the time of Jacob's trouble" (Jer. 30:7), the day of divine vengeance during Antichrist's superhuman oppression. In that awful midnight hour of tribulation, a godly remnant, the 144,000 elect and sealed witnesses of Israel (Rev. 7:1-8) will proclaim the glorious "gospel of the kingdom" (Matt. 24:14), crying out in the face of Antichrist's blasphemous imperial claims, "The true King-Messiah is coming! Turn to the Word of God! Search the prophetic Scriptures!"

In that terrible night of suffering and diabolical persecution the prophetic Scriptures of the Old Testament, particularly the Book of Daniel (Dan. 12:4) will be opened up. The Spirit-anointed Jewish evangelists and teachers, like the Apostle Paul, to whom the Lord had appeared "as to the child untimely born" (1 Cor. 15:8), will proclaim their advent message with tremendous zeal and clarity. *They* are the "wise" that "shall shine as the brightness of the firmament." They are those who in winning great numbers of their fellow-Israelites to faith in the soon-coming Christ are said to "turn many to righteousness." These shall shine in the black night of that fearful tribulation era "as the stars forever and ever" (Dan. 12:3).

The radiance of God's world-wide missionaries in that future evil hour will be like the shining of God's true witnesses in any age. However, it will be so arrestingly bright because the night will be so impenetrably black. But the night of sin is also now grossly dark. The Holy Spirit is issuing a call for believers to be radiantly filled with the Spirit, that, in this present wicked world, they may, too, be "wise" and "shine as the brightness of the firmament" and turn many to righteousness, that they may "shine as the stars *forever and ever.*"

Forever and ever! That means the glory of serving and witnessing for God in this world is only an incipient glory. It is like a flower that is only in bud, not yet opened or in full bloom. Eternity alone will bring the fruition and reward of godly living.

"Beloved, *now* are we children of God, and it is

not yet made manifest *what we shall be."* But we know that when "he shall be manifested, we shall *be like him;* for we shall see him as he is" (1 John 3:2). "When Christ, who is our life, shall be manifested, then shall ye also with him be manifested *in glory"* (Col. 3:4).

"Manifested in glory!" "Shining as the brightness of the firmament—as the stars forever and ever!" A place being prepared for us! "The Father's house of many mansions!" Who can begin to imagine the glories of the redeemed throughout the coming age and on into eternity. Who can begin to conceive the splendors God is reserving for His faithful apostles and martyrs —for those who, because of their loyalty to Jesus Christ and the Word of God "had trial of mockings and scourgings, yea, moreover of bonds and imprisonment" (Heb. 11:36).

What shall be the verdict in that day concerning those who were "stoned . . . sawn asunder . . . tempted"—those who were "slain with the sword," who "went about in sheepskins, in goatskins" who were "destitute, afflicted, ill-treated (of whom the world was not worthy)", "who wandered in deserts and mountains and caves, and the holes of the earth"? (Heb. 11:36-38).

Their verdict shall be, from the lips of the Lord Jesus Christ Himself, the Lord of Glory, and before the assembled, illimitable light-arrayed hosts of the universe, and to the shame and everlasting confusion of their tormenters, persecutors and murderers:

"Open the gates of glory to my faithful servants! They have fought a good fight! They have finished their course! They have kept the faith!

"Fling wide the portals of rest and reward to my weary pilgrims! Through the night of adversity and sin they have glimpsed my lamps of love and mercy! They have loved the light and kept the trail when the climb was steep and the darkness impenetrable.

"Through perils and temptations, through persecutions and privations, through suffering and toil, they have walked in the starlit paths provided for pilgrim feet!

"They shall be radiant as the brightness of the firmament! They shall shine as the stars forever and ever!"

I am thinking today of that beautiful land,
*   I shall reach when the sun goeth down;*
When through wonderful grace by my Savior I stand,
*   Will there be any stars in my crown?*

In the strength of the Lord let me labor and pray,
*   Let me watch as a winner of souls;*
That bright stars may be mine in the glorious day,
*   When His praise like the sea billow rolls.*

Oh, what joy it will be when His face I behold,
*   Living gems at His feet to lay down;*
It would sweeten my bliss in the city of gold,
*   Should there be any stars in my crown.*

Will there be any stars, any stars in my crown
When at evening the sun goeth down?
  When I wake with the blest
  In the mansions of rest
Will there be any stars in my crown?

Eliza E. Hewitt